Compassion Magic

TURNING TRAGEDY INTO TRIUMPH

Virginia Hunter Sampson

HUGO HOUSE PUBLISHERS, LTD.

Compassion Magic: Turning Tragic into Triumph

ISBN: 978-1-936449-92-7

Library of Congress Control Number: 2016935670

Cover Design: Chrissy Carpenter, www.freshdezigns.com

Interior Layout: Ronda Taylor, www.taylorbydesign.com

Hugo House Publishers, Ltd.
Denver, Colorado
Austin, Texas
www.HugoHousePublishers.com

Dedication

*To my children who have loved and supported me
in ways I never thought possible.*

Contents

Introduction

I'M NOT ALONE WHEN I SAY THAT MY LIFE HAS BEEN DIFFICULT. THERE have been many times in my life when I felt like a victim, angry, unloved, depressed and believed the world was against me. As a result of those experiences I shut myself off from my emotions, from others, and I became angry, bitter, and cynical.

I grew up seeing the world as a place where I either succeeded or failed as measured by our culture's standards of absolute right and wrong. I saw other people as competition. I judged myself and others constantly and harshly. This way of thinking caused me to find the world a very hostile place.

When I reached my middle-aged years, I became weighed down with a sense of failure and regret. I blamed myself and so many others for the unhappy place in which I found myself. In hopes of escaping and changing all of this in the future I decided to revisit the seminal events of my life. I searched for threads or themes that might have changed the outcome of my life ever so slightly.

I thought it was an issue of choices. If I had only made better choices in partners, careers, or any other significant events, the outcome of my life would have been significantly changed. What I discovered, to my amazement, was that one of the key elements, and perhaps the key element missing from my life, was compassion.

I always believed I was compassionate toward others, but I discovered it was really pity and judgment masquerading as compassion or it was a way of disregarding my own needs entirely negating self-compassion and creating bitterness. I was never compassionate toward myself because that would make me selfish and narcissistic or so I thought.

As I revisited my life I discovered that, at some of the lowest times in my life, there were some wonderful, caring people who showed me compassion. But I failed to recognize or appreciate them and what they gave me at the time. When my most recent marriage fell apart, something clicked. As I started down the same worn path of bitterness, I realized that I was going down a path of no return. I didn't want to hate life. I had four grown children with whom I had survived hell. I had many good things to offer this world.

So I made a decision. I could continue down the path of shame, blame, and regret, or I could find a way out of my "dark night of the soul." I began to look back over my life, and wondered what could I have done differently—what could I have asked for, and maybe what could I have been more receptive to.

As I looked back, I recognized that when some caring soul did something out of the goodness of their heart, it was compassion. Because compassion is present when we see the suffering of another and want to help alleviate that suffering. I thought, "What if?" What if during the darkest times, I had been more receptive to compassion and more willing to be compassionate with others and myself? Because compassion was absent from my life—in large part because I wasn't always willing or able to let it work its magic, it made the road I traveled ever so much more difficult and isolating.

Having to confront painful memories was hard. I took to writing them because, through the flow of words, I couldn't turn away from the pain and heartache etched in my memory. I had to write it. And as I wrote, I realized that I had been on an incredible journey, one that has led me to a place far more peaceful than I could have ever imagined. What I discovered I had to share: if we don't feel, we can't heal. If we don't heal, we are doomed to seek the same experience. When we are shut off from our own pain we are shut off from the pain of others.

Recognizing that we all have and share heartache and pain through similar experiences connects us to each other. When we identify with the heartache and pain of others, we naturally want to help alleviate that pain because we know firsthand how debilitating it can be.

When we judge and criticize ourselves and others we create barriers between us that thwart any effort to find compassion in ourselves for ourselves and others. This creates a disconnect within ourselves as we focus on the bad parts of ourselves, the parts that lead to our failures instead of our whole self.

As I reviewed my life I realized that had I practiced compassion for myself and others my difficult times would have been so much less difficult and lonely. As I wrote, I relived those parts of my life showing compassion for myself and others. I stopped framing myself and my life in terms of failure or success or absolute right or wrong.

I discovered that compassion is a great replacement for failure and absolute right/wrong, and I starting using that as my guiding principle for my life. I know now that compassion is the springboard for so many good things that enhances happiness like community/connectedness, forgiveness and gratitude.

I am still learning to be compassionate with myself. I treat myself kindly and stop constantly and harshly judging myself. I can forgive myself for my many failings which has allowed me to be open about myself and my shortcomings. I can finally abandon the fantasy of perfectionism and moral superiority. It's okay to make mistakes and not be perfect. This has opened a whole new way of seeing the world for me.

But more importantly, as I learn and practice compassion for myself, I am able to practice it with others. I can put myself in another's place and I can understand their pain and choices and forgive them for the wrongs I believed they committed against me. I can accept them as human like I am learning to accept myself. I can stop judging them and instead accept and connect with them as we all struggle on this human journey.

There is a magic to compassion. It helps anyone who finds it heal old hurts, alleviate anger, loneliness, and soothe that horrible sinking feeling of being unloved and lonely. Best of all, it creates a world that is not fraught with difficulties and heartache, one that is at least less competitive, judgmental, and hostile.

It was a long journey for me to find that magic, and it didn't come easily. It started at one of the darkest, saddest moments in my life, but from that came my greatest discovery so far—a world of caring, gratitude, forgiveness, and fulfilling connections.

A life of joy and fulfillment awaits all those who are willing to embark on their own journey. I hope by reading with me on my journey you are inspired to discover the magic of compassion in your life.

CHAPTER ONE

Heartache is Our Teacher...
If We Let It

I LOOKED ACROSS THE TABLE OVER THE HEADS OF THE TWO LAWYERS. Our eyes met and I felt a huge surge of love flowing in both directions and then a wave of despair rolled over me. Wasn't it only yesterday when we looked across at each other in a very different setting with a huge surge of love? Eight years seems like yesterday when you are in your fifties. I had just seen our wedding photos. He had introduced them into evidence at the trial. I did not want to cry here in front of him, the judge, and the lawyers. It was difficult to hold back the tears as my lawyer began to ask me the questions that are a prerequisite to the granting of a divorce.

The love was still there and at that moment it felt as strong as it had on our wedding day. Why hadn't we, he and I, been able to build on that powerful feeling of love to create a fulfilling and lasting relationship? I wanted to shout to the judge, "Stop! We still love each other!" We could still make a go of it. It had to be a mistake if that feeling could last through all of the acrimony of the last two years. What if we just changed a few things—then it would work. I forgot. We, or at least I, had already tried all of those things. Then the reality set in. It was over. The feeling of despair swept over me like the force of a powerful wind. I felt like I swayed from the power of that force. I leaned back in the chair for support.

He had already moved onto another relationship. It was eerily similar to what we had shared, at least outwardly. When I heard this I felt a huge wave of jealousy and I was angry with myself for having that feeling. As if feelings can be bad! But I was raised with that maxim. By this time, I understood that we can't control our feelings, only our response to them. But of course, that went out of my head in the power of the moment. He was a creep, a cad. He had used me. How could I be stupid enough to still have feelings for him? Love—in whatever way shape or form—is such a mystery.

I wanted to reconnect, even if just for a few moments, after the judge announced that we were divorced. We had actually connected briefly a little earlier. I was sitting in a small conference room with my lawyer waiting for the trial to begin. The door opened. "Can I talk to you alone?" he asked, but it was his eyes that pleaded with me to let him in. "This was probably just another con or so," I thought. I hadn't seen him or spoken to him in over six months. Any contact was too acrimonious, so I stopped communicating. I finally accepted that this marriage would never end in even a remotely amicable fashion. So I was very surprised when he poked his head in the door. I signaled to my lawyer that it was okay. She left the room reluctantly.

His voice and demeanor were so soft and loving that I couldn't help but respond. It was such a complete contrast to the anger and animosity of our communications of the past two years. We sat and talked in the conference room adjacent to the courtroom in the intimate way married people can and do. It amazed me how easily we slipped back into that mode. He asked about my children. I asked about his. We asked about each other's parents. He started talking to me about his new life and business. I wondered to myself why I was listening. What did I care about his new life and why would he think I would care? Still I listened. I found myself listening intently, asking questions, caring if he was happy. He confided in me. We had a history of experiences and connections that were unique to the two of us. We relived that connection if only for a few minutes. But I was better now at distinguishing between his lies and his truth. I needed to engage my brain to remind me that no matter how I felt at this moment, this relationship was over. It was not good for me even though he was right now acting like the person I had fallen in love with. He was at his best but, as in the past, circumstances would call up the worst in him. (That is not to say that was not also true for me.)

I knew that a part of Warren was trying to tap into that connection in order to get a good deal in the divorce but it still felt good to connect again. After a few moments we had nothing else to say to each other. He said what he really came to say—a dollar amount he wanted from me to settle the divorce. I nodded and said, "Let me talk to my lawyer." He tried to get me to agree without her but I resisted. He silently left the room. As I waited for my lawyer to return, I was struck by the irony of it all. The most intimate relationship in the world was boiling down to a business decision about money.

Stress was Warren's Achilles' heel. Stress brought out the worst in his personality as, I think, it does everyone. Just like pain, some people have a lower tolerance to stress. For him stress was created by anything that didn't go his way. He couldn't adapt. That forced me to unconsciously work to create a world for him where everything went his way. It was exhausting, and I lost myself in the process. It seems the more I compromised and the harder I tried, the less he tried. Could I have forced him to compromise more by being more unyielding myself, or would it just have sped up the inevitable demise of the relationship? The seeds of the end were planted at the very beginning. Here we were at the legal end. I so wanted it to be the emotional end as well.

How did I contribute to the demise of the relationship? Did I just make a lousy choice at the beginning and nothing I did or said would have changed the eventual outcome? Or did I make choices along the way that shaped the nature of the relationship and led us to this bitter end? Is it a little of both? After three marriages and four children, you would think I would have something sorted out in the relationship department. I don't. I am a total failure. My mother never misses an opportunity to remind me that I have been married three times. Her first question after I attended my twenty-fifth high school reunion was, "Did you tell them you have been married three times?" I wanted to say, "No, but at the next reunion why don't I wear a T-shirt that has "I

HAVE BEEN MARRIED THREE TIMES" emblazoned on it?" You know it would be a more modern version of what Hester Prynne wore.

I held on too long to this marriage because I didn't want to face another failure. Then I realized I was on the downward slope of my life, and I started asking myself how many unhappy years are enough or too much? I was acutely aware that I didn't know how many I may have left. I didn't want to squander them. I didn't have time to waste. So I filed for divorce.

He seemed anxious to return to his new relationship and busy life, I suspect—maybe hoped—that helped him bury the pain if he felt, if any.

"Is the marriage irretrievably broken?" my lawyer asked me as I testified from the witness box. I couldn't concentrate on the questions my lawyer was asking me. I was overwhelmed by a sense of failure and emptiness. "Oh God, I am in my fifties and I still can't get anything right! I am so tired of it all!" I said to myself. I wanted to scream that this is too painful to bear and that I don't deserve this. Instead I said, "Can you repeat the question, please?"

As I testified, he continued to look at me with that same loving look he had in the conference room. I was frantically searching for some way to get through this time on the witness stand with some dignity. Tears were welling up in my eyes. In an effort to cope, I visualized myself turning around and staring full-on into a black hole, the emptiness and loneliness of the broken connection and saying, "I am not afraid. I will get through this." That helped. I have learned that the fear of an event is often much worse than the actual event itself.

"Counsel, if you present me with the divorce decree, tomorrow I will sign it," the judge pronounced. "You are excused," he said to me in the witness box. The pronouncement felt like an execution—at least of the relationship. We gathered up our papers and left the courtroom. The bailiff locked the courtroom door behind us. The closing of the door and the clicking of the lock resonated with me. It was like the door to our relationship was forever closed and locked, but unfortunately, not forgotten.

Warren ran ahead and hurriedly got into the elevator alone. He had many important things to get back to, or at least that is the impression he wanted to give me. I walked more slowly, discussing and dissecting with my lawyer what had happened that day from a legal standpoint. This settlement had come as a complete surprise to both of us. The halls of the courthouse, along with my soul, echoed with emptiness as the bailiffs shooed away the last few occupants of the building.

I was alone when I left the courthouse. This was it. This was the end to a beautiful beginning which had been so full of promise and love that even after all the intense animosity of the past years, my composure was shattered thinking of it. I kept telling myself how stupid I was to feel that way, but that didn't help me regain my composure or feel less pain. I felt that heartache was my enemy right then. I was hurt, angry, and bitter. But I came to learn that heartache is our friend, a great teacher if we only let ourselves feel it.

Warren and I had met in the most glamorous of ways. We were both on the same tour of Italy. Is there any place that evokes more of an image of romance than Italy? I was a widow. He was separated with a divorce pending. I was so lonely, but then I think I have always been lonely. Learning to connect to others through the magic of compassion has been the most powerful antidote to loneliness I could have ever asked for—but I didn't recognize that when I met Warren.

It was the first night of the tour and we were having one of those obnoxious get-acquainted dinners. I wanted to skip it, but my sister, with whom I was traveling, insisted we attend. My sister and I arrived a little bit late, as we were out doing some sightseeing on our own. As we walked down the stairs into the dining room, my sister spied an open table. She nodded to me that we should sit there. Warren was seated there with his daughter. I can remember so clearly that evening more than ten years ago. Memories are something over which we have no control. So many things I want to remember I can't. So many things I want to forget I can't. I remember thinking that he was grumpy. The conversation was uneventful, and we parted for the evening.

For some reason he struck a nerve with me. I should have known better. Didn't I tell friends when we discussed relationships that if you felt an overpowering attraction for someone you should run the other way? We sat next to each other on the tour bus. We stood together listening to lectures about art and history in magnificent churches and museums. The attraction was palpable. We were always close enough to touch but resisting the urge. Italy is such a romantic country, and it prodded and coaxed us into a full blown romance! We sat on a bench, in front of St. Mark's Cathedral, under the magnificent night sky of Venice, and kissed. This was a perfect beginning, or so I thought.

We liked the same things. He had the same dream for his future as I did. He was attentive, polite, and solicitous. I remember thinking that a relationship would be easier this time because we were older and more mature. We each knew who we were and what we wanted. We had resolved a lot of our emotional issues we had when we were younger. After all fate had brought us together, hadn't it? I was supposed to be on a different tour but, due to a mix up at the travel agency, I ended up on the same tour with him.

After fourteen wonderful days in Italy, it was back to the grinding routine of everyday life for me, but now I had wonderful memories of romance and Italy. I returned to two teenagers with serious emotional and behavioral issues over the loss of their father, a toddler who would never know his father, a dependable eldest child who was going away to college, a career put on hold—maybe permanently as a result of having been the primary caregiver for a terminally ill spouse—and loneliness, grief, and pain over the loss of a much-loved husband to a brutal and vicious disease.

You see, my husband, Brian, had died just two years before I took my trip to Italy. My parents had agreed to come stay with my children so I could take the trip to Italy with my sister. They knew that I needed a break. The loss of my husband, Brian, had created an aching loneliness and vast emptiness—a black hole, as I image a black hole in space is, based on the little science I know. It was an inky darkness totally devoid of any light. The loneliness that had been part of my formative childhood years grew to infinite proportions with his death. It was suffocating and omnipresent. This love that blossomed in Italy with Warren was to be a light in that black hole, and it was going to flood that black hole with light. We often seek relationships, especially marriages, as a bulwark against loneliness. My relationship with Brian had been a tonic against loneliness. But I know from personal experience that is not always the case. It is also true that the loneliest I have ever been was in an unhappy marriage.

I had given Warren my phone number before we parted in Italy. I didn't hear from him when I returned home. We were living in different states at the time. I knew he stayed to travel longer in Europe, so I was patient—somewhat. Patience in relationships is not one of my virtues. This waiting probably fueled that adolescent feeling that we were meant to be together because we had such chemistry. Surely fate had placed us on the same bus tour and at the same table. About two weeks after my return he called to say he had lost my phone number. A year or so later we married and moved to California. Beautiful California beckoned with the promise of a new life, love, and career. The allure was intoxicating. We moved into a beautiful new home. He started a new business.

It all disappeared as magically as it appeared. I don't believe the death of a romance takes longer than the birth of one, but certainly the recognition that it has died does. Romance is such a wonderful fantasy and fairytale. For some people it turns into real love or at least a solid relationship. It seems in emotionally unhealthy people that the unhealthy parts are attracted to each other like magnets. Perhaps some people just get lucky and their unhealthy parts match up so well. I have never been so lucky.

"Everyone has their issues or problems, don't they? None of us is perfect. The minute things don't go our way, we can't walk away, can we?" I would say to myself on a regular basis as I struggled in my marriage to Warren. I understood the hard times of a relationship, but I didn't understand what the good times should feel like. I knew romance would fade, but what would replace it? My childhood experience observing my parents was of no use. My previous relationships were more about hard times than good times. I had the skills to navigate the hard times but not the good times. What does a good relationship look like for me? Sadly, I still have no idea. Is it one of those things you know only when it happens? In that case, I may never know because with three strikes, I am out.

I called Warren on his cell phone after I left the courthouse. He answered. We talked more about his life. He talked of including me in his new life with an offer to play some part in one of his new business ventures. I think we both knew that would never happen, but we discussed it anyway. We talked for thirty minutes or so, and I hung up only when I reached my friends' house where I was to have dinner. He called me back about an hour later while I was still at my friends' house. I didn't answer the phone. My friends wouldn't understand. He didn't leave a message.

My friends wanted to go out and celebrate the granting of the divorce. I couldn't stop crying. He and I had loved each other very much at one time, or at least I thought we did. I was hurt and sad over that loss and yes, I was bitter too. I would come to discover the healing power of compassion, but that was in my future still.

The bitterness would fade when I realized that you can only be bitter if you blame someone other than yourself for a situation. I have acquired at least enough maturity and experience to realize that I am responsible for the present situation. I made the choices that brought me here. I alone am to blame, not him. He could only be who he is. I could not expect him to be otherwise. Sure, he could have changed if he wanted to, but he didn't want to. His number-one priority was getting what he wanted, and I was a means to that end. When I stopped serving that purpose, the relationship was over.

"Maybe we can celebrate another day," I said to my friends. I didn't go anywhere else after I left my friends. I stayed home so I could cry with no one watching. I wanted to wail at the injustice. There seems to be something so wrong about celebrating the end of a beautiful beginning.

I haven't spoken to nor heard from Warren since the day the divorce was granted. I am thankful for that.

We label so much in our society e.g. divorces, job losses, broken relationships, and more as failures. Labeling events as failures allows us to manage them and engage in a mental mission to fix them, at least outwardly. We think, "If only," if only we had done things differently or made a different choice, we could have avoided this failure. So we beat ourselves up with regrets and what ifs. It is endless.

In the days following my divorce, I would look in the mirror. I saw the image of a middle-aged woman staring back at me. When did that happen? I wondered. The image reminded me of the passage of so many years. It frightened me that so much of my life is now behind me.

I can deal with this divorce from Warren, I told myself. Haven't I proven in the past that I am a survivor?

But as I looked at myself in the mirror, I thought, "Are we only here to survive our life, or is there real joy to be experienced?" It was a turning point. I realized that I could just continue to barely survive, embittered, or I could find ways to experience joy in my life no matter what.

It was kind of an aha moment. So what if much of my life was now behind me? I did not want to repeat the unhappy patterns of my past years and squander my remaining years. To make that happen, I had to change the way I saw myself and my life. My usual *modus operandi* of beating myself up over my failures and then being weighed down with regret and self-recrimination hadn't helped me to lead a happier life.

I would have to dig deep and be really honest with myself to find a way out of the abyss of my repeated patterns of unhealthy behavior or mistakes, as we like to call them.

My first realization: what if those constant feelings of regret and failure are only unresolved heartache and hurt when things didn't go the way I wanted, or thought they should, or God help us, the way society said they should be?

In that moment, I allowed just a tiny bit of self-compassion, some kindness toward myself, to seep into the cracks of pain I was feeling. It was the salve I needed to start healing. I now realize there are major lessons to learn from the heartache of failure which lead to a much better way to view our failures.

We run away from heartache and try everything we can to avoid experiencing the awful pain of heartache and loss. We stay incredibly busy occupying ourselves virtually every waking moment, rushing from one daily task to another or being engaged in some mind-numbing activity like endless TV watching. We blame ourselves. We blame others. We become bitter. We become angry and depressed. We believe everyone is happier and more successful than we are. We stop experiencing real joy in our life. At least that is what I have done in my life. But that once small slice of self-compassion helped me realize that if I can't feel pain, I can't feel joy.

Once I let myself be compassionate towards my own failures, even just a little, I realized that if I want to quiet those constant negative voices and find peace in my life as it is, I'm going to have to heal the unresolved heartaches. There would be no easy way to do this, I told myself. Since the superfluous ways didn't work, I would have to embark on the arduous task of reliving my heartaches to actually experience all the pain, disappointment and hurt. If I didn't, those unresolved heart-aches would continue to interfere with my happiness and the heartache of my recent divorce would turn into anger, bitterness, and cynicism.

My first step would be to stop referring to events in my life as failures but rather as heartaches. It would not be easy to retrain my mind but, once I started, I could see that labeling events as failures only resulted in me constantly evaluating, judging, and criticizing myself—and others.

Failure implies there is a perfect standard or way of doing things, and if I'm a failure, then I have missed that mark. With that realization came some clarity. I could see that seeing events as failures was a legacy of my childhood. But how could I unlearn that?

It seems to me that framing the world in terms of failure/success and absolute right/wrong had contributed greatly to my unhappiness. But what replaces those standards? In the days that followed my revelation about self-compassion, I vowed to look back over my life and try to find the threads that contributed to or created what I am searching for: peace from berating myself, a sense of positive well-being, even joy, and connections to others to ease the loneliness I have always felt.

Heartache is a great teacher. It is also the catalyst to discovering compassion for ourselves and others. Compassion is indispensable if we want to live a happy, fulfilling, and satisfying life, but only when you practice it towards yourself can you open yourself up to give compassion to others and to receive it from them as well.

CHAPTER TWO

A Relationship Unravels

"I WANT TO COME HOME. CAN YOU SEND ME SOME MONEY TO BUY A ticket?" I said to my mother from a payphone. I was in California staying with my soon-to-be husband, David. We could not afford a phone as David had run up a huge phone bill he couldn't pay. My parents never asked why I didn't have a phone. They never asked anything about my life at all then or ever. My mother wired the money. In the meantime, I changed my mind. I can't remember why. Maybe I couldn't decide which was less welcoming—my old home with my mother or my new one with my soon-to-be husband. If only I had possessed the wherewithal to strike out on my own. I can't even remember entertaining that as an option.

As I look back on it that was such an obvious choice. This was the late seventies and I still viewed myself in the roles of my mother—as traditional wife and mother. I did not see myself as an independent working woman. That was a job forced on me later by circumstances but not something I really wanted. I was just about to finish college. I had no sense of direction other than getting married. I am embarrassed to admit that, but it is true. "Don't ever do that to us again," my mother reprimanded me when I called later to say I wasn't going to come home. That was all that was ever said about the incident with my mother. I never spoke to my father about it. My mother handled "those matters" in their marriage.

In this instance the voice of prudence did whisper in my ear that perhaps marrying David was not a good idea, but I ignored it. I was infatuated, and I had absolutely no idea how to discern infatuation from love. I didn't even know there was a difference. One of my friends told me he was lucky because his infatuation turned into love. I was not so lucky. If I was not so impatient I might have discovered the difference or at least been able to see David rationally. I was impatient to find love or get married or something else. We married soon after that incident and had three children.

Have you ever noticed that unhappiness just kind of creeps up on you like vines growing on a trellis? A vine starts with gentle tendrils. The tendrils grow large and strong and become vines. If left alone, without any pruning or tending, these vines will warp and eventually break the trellis. So it is that little tendrils of unhappiness ever so surreptitiously start clinging to our soul. Some unhappiness is good as it helps us to grow and mature. However, those tendrils of unhappiness can grow and grow until, if left unattended, they choke your soul. This is not sorrow. Sorrow is palpable and real. It makes itself known. This is not real depression. Depression has you totally in its grip. It is the grip of someone unwilling to forgive him or herself, and so when those vines choke their soul, they don't realize it is of their own making.

Unhappiness is insidious. It is so easily disguised or explained as a momentary response to a temporary, unfortunate situation. It can be so easily ignored. It is so very dangerous because we can become accustomed to that emotional state and we stop being able to recognize when momentary unhappiness grows and becomes something more. We must always keep our finger on the pulse of our happiness or the tendrils of unhappiness will become vines and choke us. We must prune and tend. I let my unhappiness go for far too long. By the time I realized how unhappy I was, it had much too strong a hold on me. Pruning and tending were ineffective. I had to tear the vine out by its roots, and in the process I was irrevocably damaged.

"Mom, Mom," Jessica greeted me at the door when I arrived home from the office. It was about seven o'clock p.m. I had left for the office around seven that morning. It was the day after Christmas. Usually all the children came to greet me at the door when I arrived home. Today they didn't.

There was an eerie silence in the house. "Where are Ellen and Samuel? Where is your dad?" I asked Jessica. She was clinging to me silently with her head buried in my stomach. "David, Ellen, Samuel," I called out. No one answered. "Jessica, you have to let go of me," I said.

Jessica finally looked up at me and said, "Mom, Dad broke all of Samuel's toys with a baseball bat. He smashed them to pieces!"

I started up the stairs to Samuel's bedroom. I could see that the door to his room was closed. Jessica was still clinging to my waist. I felt like I was going to throw up. I pushed open the door to Samuel's bedroom. Broken pieces of toys covered the floor. The ramp to the Hot Wheels garage he had just excitedly opened yesterday was in pieces on the floor in the middle of the room. I recognized other pieces of toys he had received for Christmas just yesterday.

I was now calling frantically for Ellen and Samuel. David was nowhere to be found, or so it seemed. I walked next door into Ellen's room. She and Samuel were seated together on the floor playing with some of her toys. None of her toys were broken.

I hugged and kissed them, and then I went looking for David. He was in our bedroom. "How could you do that? You are crazy! You need to get out of the house right now!" I shouted at him. He said nothing. I shouted at him a while longer. He still said and did nothing. He just stared at me blankly.

In emulating my upbringing, I went downstairs and fixed dinner for the children and me. At dinner I talked a little bit but, for the most part, we ate in silence. We didn't discuss what happened. I had Jessica do her homework. I bathed the younger two and put them to bed. Samuel slept in Ellen's room that night as I was too exhausted to clean his room. I will do it tomorrow night, I said to myself. I closed the door to Samuel's room and told the children to stay out of there. I fell into bed. I convinced myself that it was better to maintain some order and predictably after such an ordeal. But it was as if David had smashed our marriage to pieces that night along with the toys. I closed the door on the relationship that night as I closed the door to Samuel's room with the broken toys in it. I knew then that I would file for divorce. The marriage had been broken for a long time.

There was no point in trying to talk to David about anything that happened or needed to happen including that night. He and I would talk or more accurately I would talk, make plans or make a decision and then when things didn't go as planned, he would tell me he never agreed to that or that everything was my fault. He would also simply deny he ever behaved in a certain way. I started to doubt myself. It was actually stronger than that. I felt totally disoriented again—a feeling I had all the time the last months of living with David. Was I going crazy? Was the stress affecting me that much? Why did I even bother to say anything to him? I knew that nothing was ever going to change with him. He would never admit he made a mistake or did anything wrong. How does the person in whom you can confide your deepest secrets become the last person in the world you can or would talk to?

"Get out," I told David again the day after he had smashed the toys. I said it every day for weeks after that. He simply ignored me. He pretended nothing out of the ordinary had happened. How can he do that? It made me feel like I was crazy. Was I imagining what happened? I knew Jessica had seen it, and that gave me comfort and strength. I couldn't afford to move anywhere with the children. I didn't have the money for the deposits needed to move into an apartment. I didn't have money to go to a hotel. I didn't have money to hire a lawyer, and I am not sure that would have helped if I did. The next several months passed without any further incidents of violence. Eventually the violence returned with even more force, but it was now directed at me. I don't think the children really knew the difference.

"You are out of control. You are crazy!" I yelled at him.

"You make me do the things I do because you are such a lousy wife!" David shouted as he hurled something at me. I ran in the direction of one of the bedrooms. He followed me. I turned to face him in the doorway of the bedroom. He punched me, and I fell down. Samuel was standing behind me, and he fell too. I landed on top of Samuel. He was five years old.

I got up and tried to leave the room. "You are not going anywhere," David said to me. He stood between me and the door. He wouldn't let me leave the room, much less the house. Every time I tried to leave, he pushed me back into the room. I tried not to scare the kids more than they already were scared. I heard the kids in the next room playing together. They came in and said good night to me.

The next day, David got Samuel and Jessica off to school. Ellen went next door to the sitter's house. Eventually David dragged me into the car with him on some errands. He stopped for a red light. I jumped out of the car. I was fortunately only a few blocks from the office. I can't really remember what I said or did at the office. I know I really didn't tell anyone what had happened. I was too embarrassed. Somehow I got a ride back to the house. I called the police. David didn't come back to the house that night.

A police officer arrived at the house. He stood at the door looking at me with a mixture of annoyance and outright disgust. "We can't do anything, ma'am, since your husband isn't at home. If he comes back give us a call," the police officer said to me.

"You mean I have to wait for him to commit more acts of violence before you can do anything?" I exclaimed. The officer just shrugged his shoulders, turned, and walked away.

I went to work the next day. The children went to school and the sitter. The children were understandably acting out at home. I was feeling totally overwhelmed. I called a few family lawyers, but I didn't have the money to hire one. That night David came home again. The next time David became violent and tried to keep me in the house, I was able to run out the front door and get to my neighbors. My neighbor called the police. I ran back home immediately to see David pulling out of the driveway with Samuel in the back seat of the car. My heart sank.

"Do you have someplace you can go for the night?" the police officer asked me. He had come into the house to check things out and was standing next to me with a kind and concerned look on his face. Finally, I was talking to a compassionate officer who didn't look at me like I had horns. Domestic violence wasn't taken very seriously by police officers or even the courts back then. I frantically searched in my mind for someone to call. We had just moved to this city several months ago. This isn't exactly something you want to talk to good friends about, much less new acquaintances. "You need to call someone," he insisted. Since David had fled before the officer arrived there was nothing that could be done to him right then.

"What about my son? He needs to bring him back right now!" I said to the officer.

"He is your son's father and there is no custody order, so I can't do anything about him taking the boy," the officer said.

Very reluctantly I picked up the phone and dialed the person I knew the best in my new city.

"Eva, can the kids and I stay at your house tonight?" I heard myself ask. I felt like I was outside my body—like I was watching this happen to someone else. I knew Eva was going to ask why, and I dreaded that. She did and I responded, "David has hit me and tried to keep me from leaving the house. The police officer does not want the children and me to stay here tonight."

Eva hung up the phone without saying anything. "We will be all right here," I told the officer. I spent the entire evening in a panic wondering where Samuel was, and if he was okay. David dropped Samuel off at the house later that night and left. Maybe things are going to get better I thought.

Soon after that I had a restraining order issued against David. The process of obtaining the restraining order was humiliating. The courts and judges were not particularly sympathetic to domestic violence victims, especially well-educated ones. The fact that I was well-educated made it even more embarrassing. I didn't have any police reports to corroborate my story. I sensed that they thought I was making it all up—a hysterical woman. There was no self-help available through the courts like they have now where you can obtain forms and instructions on how to do everything yourself. I was totally on my own, or so I felt. I could never get David served with the restraining order, so it was of no use. During that time, I think he would have simply ignored it anyway. I filed for divorce without a lawyer. By some miracle David simply stopped coming back to stay at the house. That didn't mean he disappeared from our lives entirely.

I kept the violence and divorce a secret from people at the office. I was afraid if I told people at the office, I would get fired; maybe not right then, but at some point in time it would happen. The partners at the firm had already alluded to the fact that they were unhappy I was getting a divorce and gave me a look that meant I must not let anything in my personal life interfere with my productivity at work.

I eventually was able to talk about what was going on with my friend at work, Martha. She knew something serious was going on and kept asking until one day I couldn't hold back any longer. We were pretty new friends, but still she cared. She listened. She offered to help. She didn't judge me. She showed me compassion. Without her I'm not sure I could have made it through the violence and despair. She was one of the only bright spots in my very bleak world. I tried to tell a few others, but I tested the waters and decided it would be unwise. I told a few of the parents of my children's friends that I was going through a divorce, and the reaction was not pleasant. I didn't want them to forbid their children to play with mine, and I thought that was real possibility, so I did not share further. They looked at me with disgust and condemnation. Certainly I was a failure and a bad person because I could not save my marriage.

I never asked them to, but I know that the children kept everything a secret as well. We were an isolated island of misery and despair surrounded by and functioning in a huge ocean of normalcy at least for others. I went to work. The children went to school. We carried on as if our life was not all about fear and violence. I felt disconnected, as if I lived in two separate worlds. I had no idea how to help the children cope other than trying to maintain routine and normalcy to our lives. The children and I didn't talk about what was going on. I coped with the situation the way I knew how. I know now that was a huge mistake. The violence continued.

The phone was ringing again. I looked at the clock. It was two in the morning. "Who are you sleeping with tonight, you whore?" I heard David scream. I hung up the phone. I double-checked to make sure all the windows and doors were locked. I lay awake all night. I was afraid if I didn't answer the phone he would come over to the house and do something worse. David picked up my mail from the mailbox and read it. He broke into the house, answered my phone and ransacked my things. He stole my car. He called me at the office and at home accusing me of having affairs with every man I came into contact with.

"I am going to kill you, cut your body up into little pieces, and bury it in the desert so no one will find you. I am going to kidnap the kids and take them to Mexico," David spewed this venom. He had barged his way into the house on the pretense of picking up the children for a visit. Suddenly he stopped. Jessica had entered the room. It had become a pattern that was repeated over and over again. He would say these things every time I had contact with him. Each time Jessica would enter the room, David would stop. I know Jessica heard what he said. My poor Jessica! I was afraid David would really carry out his threats. I think Jessica was too. He was crazy enough at that time to do it.

How was I supposed to respond to all this? I wasn't sure if I should fight back or be passive, hoping that would placate him. In the end, my response never affected his behavior to any significant degree. It seemed no matter what I did, he was hell bent on abusing me. Nothing could stop that. Any change that could have affected his behavior would have to have been done long before he first raised his fist to punch me. I knew he was in a rage and wanted to destroy everything. Things like courts and police have no power over such a person. That was perhaps the scariest thing of all.

As I write this, I am overcome by powerful feeling of fear, anger, and depression. I feel confused. It is as if my defenses kick in and my mind becomes foggy to protect me from too many bad memories. I have tried so hard to forget the details of what happened. I don't even want to remember them here.

This continued for at least nine months during which David engaged in all of the above and more on at least a weekly basis. The children and I lived constantly, every minute of every day, with the fear generated by him. I kept trying to keep other things as normal as possible for the children. I don't recall why I did not get more help from the courts or police. Was I right to feel bad about myself because I didn't fight back? Or should I just judge myself as a victim who is helpless to change the course of events at that particular moment? I tried not to judge myself too harshly. In some way I sensed that if I fought David too much and involved the courts and police, he would fight harder and maybe carry out one of his threats. I hoped David's rage would eventually be spent and he would simply go away.

It is difficult to imagine that attitudes were so different in the mid-eighties regarding domestic violence, but they were. The police were not sympathetic. They would come to my door after a 911 call. They would look at me in a totally disgusted manner. When I said David had fled they would simply turn and walk away. They never examined me for bruises or marks. They never even made a report. They never gave me any information about any domestic violence shelters or court remedies. The procedures to have emergency court hearings were not in place as they are now, or if they were they didn't tell me about them. I stopped calling the police because they made me feel like the scum of the earth.

Why did I marry him—David? It was obviously a poor choice, but of course I didn't recognize that at the time. The violence didn't start until the very end when the marriage was falling apart. There may have been warning signs that he was disposed to such violence, but it wouldn't have mattered to me. I would simply have ignored them. I was in love. I wanted to save David. He has his problems, but the power of my love would change him, or so I thought. It is hard to believe that I could be that stupid, but I was.

I have since learned that it is okay to want to help people, but it probably isn't something you should do when choosing a mate. Saving them isn't going to help them one bit. It is better to choose a mate with whom you can form a solid relationship so that relationship can provide the support you need to go out and help others and save the world. Crippled partners make for crippled relationships which in my experience can have disastrous consequences. I didn't practice any self-compassion in my relationship with David. I didn't set any limits or expectations for him. Compassion for our partner is great, but compassion isn't bending over backwards to allow them to continue their non-optimum behavior.

I obviously didn't know that at the time. You see, I thought was special because only *I* could understand David and see his good qualities. I would make excuses for this behavior based on his motivation or good character that only I could see. Of course this motivation and character didn't exist anywhere but in my own mind. Later in my life a friend told me, "You know how people feel about you by how they treat you." That was sadly not something I understood until much later.

I thought David and I had the right feeling for each other. My grandmother said something to me once. She said what held her and my grandfather together for fifty-plus years was the knowledge that they had the right feeling in the beginning. Well, sometimes I wish she hadn't said that to me. Even before there was a media obsession with romantic love, I had imbibed enough literature and personal lore to know that I had the right feeling for David. I was infatuated and I thought that was the right feeling.

"Please raise your right hand and be sworn," the bailiff said. I did. I was sworn in. I sat down. I looked around the courtroom. Thankfully it was almost empty. David didn't even bother to show up. I didn't really expect him to. I was relieved he hadn't fought the matter in the courts. The judge asked me a few questions. "You may step down now. If you wait, the clerk will give you a copy of the divorce decree," the judge said. That was it. Legally, it was over. Emotionally, there was still much to resolve. I moved on to the next task at hand. I had to get back to the office.

The granting of the divorce gave me some relief. David was no longer legally permitted to enter the house. That didn't really stop him, but it gave me some feeling of control. David was granted visitation rights with the children.

"I'll be over to pick up the kids to take them to a movie," David said over the phone. In my naiveté I told the children that their father would be over tomorrow to pick them up and take them to a movie. The two younger ones, Samuel and Ellen, were very excited. They were three and a half and five years old. They got dressed early and waited patiently. They were talking about what they were going to do with him and what movie they wanted to see. At least as much as kids that age can discuss those matters. I knew they were excited and, quite frankly I was looking forward to a little time to myself. I was going to sleep.

"When will Daddy be here?" Samuel asked. "We are going to miss the movie," he later complained when the time came and went for his father's arrival.

"He will be here. Something must have come up that caused a delay," I said. After an hour passed with no phone call and no knock at the door, I realized he wasn't coming. I should have said something to the children. I was a coward.

Eventually Samuel just found something else to do besides wait for him. He went to his room and played with his Matchbox cars. Ellen, who was three at the time, cried and carried on. I tried to get them interested in going out with me to a movie, but they didn't want to. Their hurt was palpable.

"How could you just not show up," I shrieked into the phone when David finally did call. I was surprised at myself because I had given up on fighting with him over how he treated me, but apparently I still had the energy and grit to fight with him over how he treated the children.

"You are crazy. I never told you that I was going to pick the kids up and take them to a movie," he responded.

"Did I misunderstand him?" I asked myself. Eventually I just wouldn't tell the children he was going to pick them up.

"We don't want to take a bath. We want to go live with our dad! We want to go live with our dad!" Ellen and Samuel were chanting. I was somewhat accustomed to hearing this by now as it had been going on since David moved out of the house. They did it even after David broke their hearts by not visiting. This chant accompanied just about every request I made of the younger two to do something they didn't want to do. I gave them a bath silently, dried them off, and got them into bed.

Most of the time, when David did show up, he would take only one of them. "I simply can't handle all three of them," or "I simply can't afford to take all of them to the movie," he would say. One very radiant child would leave with him while the other would crumple up in a ball on the floor and cry. I was left with shattered children whose pieces I tried to put back together. (Jessica, the oldest never really wanted to go with her father.)

That is how I came to view my children. They were shattered into pieces at a very young age and the rest of their lives have been about putting those pieces back together. The pieces never fit back together perfectly, but at least now all the pieces are back and in some kind of reasonable order.

The children and I were crumbling under the strain of it all. I had to do something. The violence continued.

Often when David would arrive to pick up one of the children, he would punch me in the face. He would threaten to kill me in graphic detail. My goal had been not to antagonize David in hopes of avoiding even more violence. I agonized over what to do. I didn't tell my parents about the violence. When I had tried to speak with them about difficult times, they simply did not engage. I think they had no idea how to cope so they pretended things were not happening.

I finally worked up my courage. "If you don't leave us alone, I am going to disappear in the night, and you will never ever see the children again!" I told David. I thought about this for months before I said it to David. I spent a good bit of time thinking about what state I would go to and how I would change my name so he couldn't find us. It had no effect on David. Maybe he didn't believe me.

There is no word to describe how desperate I felt. The police and courts provided no concrete help. I didn't know where to turn for help. David had an older brother, Frank, he was very close to. His brother lived in another state so they had not seen each other much in recent years, and I didn't know him that well. However, in the past, David had really looked up to his brother. We had seen him at family gatherings when we lived in the same city, but that was a number of years ago. I hadn't seen or spoken to him in a long time. I knew Frank was very protective of David from stories they both told and from seeing them interact. Should I call Frank? I kept asking myself. I had no idea how he would react. I imagined when I told him about the violence that he would call me names and hang up the phone. Still he was my last hope, so I got up my courage and called him.

"Frank, can you please speak to your brother, and get him to leave us alone?" I briefly described David's violent behavior. I really didn't go into much detail. Frank silently listened. He didn't argue with me. He didn't make any judgments about me. Frank didn't say much, but I could feel the understanding and compassion. It was the first time through the ordeal that I felt someone cared just for the sake of caring for another human being.

"I will talk to him," Frank said and hung up the phone. Shortly after that conversation, David moved back to his home state. I don't know what I would have done if Frank had not believed me or helped me. I never spoke to Frank again. He was David's brother after all and that is where his loyalty was—understandably. But I knew without a doubt that his compassion had saved me.

As part of the divorce, the court entered an order for child support. David simply ignored the court order. He never paid any child support. I wasn't surprised and really didn't much care. All I ever wanted from David was for him to leave us alone. I sensed that if I tried to enforce the child support order David would come back into our lives. The money was not worth it. Years later, when I tried to collect some child support, that is exactly what happened. I abandoned my claim forever.

Eventually David just disappeared altogether. That is what I had hoped for but not until after he had made our life a living hell for quite a long time. We were left to pick up the pieces of our shattered lives. It would be a long hard road for all of us to heal from these events.

I had met a psychologist through work. I was referred to her to help with one of the clients at the firm. She had the kindest demeanor, and I was immediately drawn to her. I battled my demons regarding how worthless I was to need help. However, I was in such a terrible state, I finally caved in and made an appointment with her. In the beginning, Dr. M. would let me show up in her office on short notice. I would race into her office, sit in the chair, and sob uncontrollably. She bore the brunt of my rage, fear, helplessness, and anxiety. She listened to me *ad nauseum.* She helped me develop some tools to deal with this situation. She was my sounding board and my support. She never judged me or criticized me or how I handled any of this. She charged me very little, if anything, because she knew I could not afford to pay. Her kindness, understanding, and compassion kept me afloat. I honestly don't think I would have made it through this dark time without her. Just knowing she was there if I needed her kept my spirits up. She was my lifeline although I am not sure I recognized her compassion at the time. I just knew I felt better and could function on some level after visiting with her.

The world seemed a very harsh and cruel place at this time in my life. I didn't get support from my family or the community. I often wonder how my children survived without being able to reach out to others. Samuel and Ellen were so young that they could only act out their pain. Samuel was disciplined at school for acting out. Jessica found solace with her friends in whom she may have confided.

As I look back over that very bleak and violent time, I realize that, at the darkest moment, someone would reach out to me. Someone would do something to help me just because I needed it. They didn't ask anything in return. I didn't recognize it fully until later but it was the compassion exhibited by almost strangers—Frank, Martha, and Dr. M.—that saved my life. I also could see that the work I had put into keeping things as normal as possible for my children was an act of compassion as well.

We need the help and support of others. We don't live on islands unto ourselves. Thirty years ago, we didn't have the support systems in place for domestic abuse survivors. Compassion for those victims is not built into the system. But institutional compassion can't ever take the place of someone, a friend, a mom, a complete stranger, saying, "Hey, what's going on?" and then being willing to listen—without judgment, without prejudice. That is when the person suffering may find that they have just a little more courage, find a little more patience, feel just a little more oomph to get through the next hurdle that life inevitably throws our way.

CHAPTER THREE

Childhood Hauntings: A Legacy of Judgment and Criticism

I CONTINUED SPORADICALLY TO SEE DR. M. AS THE DIVORCE SITUATION eased, we were able to talk about things other than the domestic violence. The domestic violence had finally ended. My ex-husband had moved out of state. Yet the heartache raged on and on. I was still in crisis mode, but I think I have always functioned in crisis mode. That is one of the legacies of my childhood.

I was sitting with my head bowed, tears streaming, snot running, shoulders shaking, sobbing uncontrollably in front of Dr. M. I was acutely aware of how embarrassed and humiliated I felt. Through my gasps for air, I heard Dr. M. say that I had stuffed down all the hurts and emotions for so long I couldn't stuff anymore. Weird what we think of at such a time of crisis. I pictured my head as the top of an erupting volcano. I envisioned the top of my head with gross stuff oozing and spurting out of it and me trying to push the stuff back down and close the lid but the stuff wouldn't stop spurting out.

"I have been betrayed!" I said through clenched teeth to Dr. M. By this time, I had calmed down a bit. I was relieved I was finally able to identify the source of some of my present pain. "I did everything I was supposed to do. I was a good girl. I got an education. I was supportive of my husband. I spend time with my children. I devote myself to my family. I put them first. I go to work every day, and I work very hard." As I talked, the level of anger escalated.

"How have you been betrayed by doing all of that?" she asked me.

"I should have a good life. I earned it. I don't deserve this life!" I shouted. "There has to be something wrong with me because bad things don't happen to good girls or good people." What had I done to deserve this? I was brimming over with rage. I felt totally alone, abandoned, empty. I had that same feeling as a child. I realize now that these feelings have waxed and waned all my life.

"Tell me about your childhood—what was it like?" I heard Dr. M. ask me. A wave of panic passed over me. "Did she really want to open that can of worms?" I thought to myself. I thought I was working with her to resolve the anger and resentment that was lingering after my divorce from David. I almost mused aloud that to look back into my childhood would be akin to taking a plunge into a black, foreboding abyss.

She must have sensed that I couldn't or didn't want to discuss my childhood. "Do I really have to talk about my childhood?" I asked. "Isn't that all behind me? I survived it. That is all that needs to be said about it, and since I can't change any of it, why bother?" I finished.

She was undaunted. She narrowed her inquiry. "Tell me about an event you remember." Another wave of panic passed over me, and my mind went blank.

"I don't have many memories of events from my childhood," I told her. She paused one of those long scary pauses when you, as the patient, think she is saying to herself, "This patient is really screwed up."

"Well, how did you feel as a child?"

The wall holding back those emotions must have burst. The tears exploded. I didn't know if I had the strength or stamina to go down that road.

I come from a long line of stoics that believe you solve all of your own problems by yourself without any help. If you just persevere and try harder things will get better. If they don't get better, it is because you didn't try hard enough. In other words, it is entirely your fault. You are weak if you seek psychological help or really any help. You don't talk about your problems. You muscle through them. In fact, I am not sure you were ever allowed to admit you even had problems or emotions for that matter. You certainly don't discuss your problems or emotions with anyone, not even, or especially, your family. You had a very limited range of emotions you could express and any expression had to be temperate and moderate. You have to suffer in order to earn the right to go to heaven. Life is about survival, not enjoyment. Women do not express anger. For men, that is the only emotion they were permitted to express. If their expression was not moderate or temperate, that is a failing but one that can be tolerated and explained away. These are some of the unwritten rules or teachings of my childhood. They shaped my world and me. I really wasn't conscious of them until I started going to therapy. They were deeply buried.

"I have to leave early today. I have a doctor's appointment," I said to one of the partners at the firm where I worked.

"Is everything all right?" he kindly asked.

"Sure," I replied. I wasn't going to tell him I was going to see a psychologist! I was embarrassed to seek help and I have kept it a secret pretty much until now. That is another legacy of my childhood—keeping secrets. My self-image, at that time, was that of the self-reliant, strong person who can handle everything and has her life together. I couldn't maintain that image if I confessed my fears and problems to someone. I couldn't let anyone see the real me—only the image. But in reality I was financially and emotionally bankrupt. I had three small children to support and care for, and I was still processing the end of a marriage with a spouse who had become physically and emotionally abusive.

"What do you remember about your childhood?" the psychologist firmly asked again. I was quiet for a time thinking I guess.

"Mostly I felt afraid—always afraid," I whispered out loud.

"You felt afraid," she repeated.

"Yes," I said. "I felt totally alone." She didn't say anything else. I hated the sympathetic look she gave me when I said that. In my family I learned that you don't want to be pitied ever! I felt the fear and loneliness welling up in me right then. It could do that—just appear at any time. Even as an adult I felt paralyzed by it. As I got older, I learned to talk myself through it, but I couldn't do that when I was a child.

By all outward appearances I had an idyllic childhood. After all, it was the fifties and sixties in a small Midwestern city. The fifties and the sixties have been so overdone that it has become tiresome to even think about it, much less write about it. It has been glorified and vilified and everything in between. It is hard to escape from all the generalizations and romanticism hoisted onto that era. What really happened is of little significance. It is our memory or perception of what happened that is most significant. The romantic veneer is dangerous as it can taint our memory of our own experiences of those times.

"NOOOO! I don't want to…," someone was screaming. I looked over to see where that horrible noise was coming from. I saw my sister crumpled up in a ball on the floor crying. My sister had a whole physical writhing act that went along with the screams and tears. She looked like she was in terrible physical pain. She was about eight years old at the time.

"Where are your shoes?" my mother screamed at my sister. My sister didn't want to wear her (ugly) orthopedic shoes that day. In fact, she never wanted to wear those ugly saddle shoes, and this was a fairly typical morning scene at our house. Usually my dad had already left for work. We were supposed to be leaving to get on the school bus. It reminded me of the scene in *The Wizard of Oz* where the wicked witch melts after Dorothy pours water on her. My mother was exceptionally hard on my sister that morning, maybe because we were going to miss the school bus. Something my mother said even triggered some tears in my eyes.

I can remember clenching my teeth and my fists and saying to myself, "She will never make me cry." To this day I have kept my promise. No one else has made me cry much either. My poor sister just didn't have the ability to withstand the abuse. As you would expect, our respective coping mechanisms have taken a toll on each of us.

Abuse comes in many forms. It wasn't so much what my mother said to my sister as how she said it. They were harmless words really, but the tone of voice, the facial expressions, and body language said it all. She didn't need to use hurtful words. Her eyes were bulging out. Her face was contorted, and her body seemed poised to strike at any moment. "You are stupid, worthless, and I hate you," she said with her eyes, voice, and her body.

Her interaction with my sister and I was always adversarial. I felt like she was my enemy. This lack of hurtful words was particularly difficult to deal with because when I would review events later in my head, I couldn't find fault with what my mother actually said. Had I imagined that my mother looked at my sister in evil ways? After all she really didn't say anything evil. In going over what happened in my mind, there was a disconnect between what objectively happened and my reaction to it. I reacted as if my mother was verbally and emotionally abusive. But she wasn't overtly or objectively abusive. This was all part of the dishonesty that shrouded everything my mother did and said. I learned not to trust my instincts. I would berate myself for thinking ill of my mother. After all, she really didn't say anything mean or strike my sister. I would decide that I imagined the meanness because I had to give my mother the benefit of the doubt. After all, she was my mother and she loved us, didn't she?

We lived in the middle class suburbs in a very small Cape Cod and later in a somewhat larger ranch-style brick house. Both houses were very small by today's standards. We had one bathroom for five people in our first house. My sister and I shared a bedroom until I was thirteen years old. We had a large yard—not fenced. (It was and maybe still is unfriendly and un-neighborly to fence in your yard in that part of the country.) They were both basic houses with no perks. My family consisted of my parents, my older brother, and younger sister. We had a dog. My mother didn't work but devoted herself to the family and community. She was actively involved in church and school committees and organizations.

My father went to work each day at the company where he would spend almost his entire working career. My mother cooked dinner every night. It was basic Midwestern fare—meat, potato or rice, and an over-cooked vegetable. We rarely had fish, and if we did it was terrible. My dad coached Little League for my brother. We—the girls—didn't have any sports until high school. We did have the Girl Scouts. My parents never fought, at least not in front of us. I had no experience with any type of illness or death as a child. With a few minor variations, everyone else's outward or physical life was the same.

"I am quitting Girl Scouts," I blurted out with my eyes shut tightly. It took weeks for me to get up the courage to tell my mother, but I finally did. I knew the consequence would be severe but I had to do it. My mother had been looking in the other direction when I said it. Her head whirled around so fast it now reminds me of the scene in the movie *The Exorcist*. She started spewing similar venom as well.

"You WHAT?!" she screeched in my direction. Now, in all fairness, I have to say that my mother was very involved in the Girl Scouts.

I took a deep breath and repeated the statement, "I am quitting Girl Scouts. Beth, (my sister) is still a Scout." I hoped this would diffuse some of her anger.

My mother screamed at me for a while as I stood silently looking at the floor. I think she told me all the things she did for me and how ungrateful, unappreciative, and selfish I was. That was the usual fare anyway. My mother liked to play the martyr. Her anger spent for the time being, she turned and left the room. All disobedience and/or disagreements were followed by a long period of stony silence and being ignored, at least when it came to me. I knew this outburst was only the beginning. There would be more. She didn't usually act this way when my father was home. I don't know if it would have mattered if she did. My father had a real ability to live in his own reality. In his world my mother didn't act like this or do these things.

"Mother, I need you to sign the permission slip and give me a check for the field trip next week," I said. She didn't look at me or acknowledge what I said. I left the field trip information on the table and left the room. (She never told me, but eventually she paid it because I was able to go on the school field trip.) If I spoke to her again, who knows what might happen. You see, only a few days had passed since I told my mother that I was quitting Girl Scouts. It would be several months before she would talk to me or even look at me. I simply didn't exist for a few months as far as she was concerned. I knew this would be the price I would pay for going against something that she wanted. To me, at the time, it was worth the battle. Sometimes she would give me hateful looks when I walked into the room. My father never noticed. This was all part of the battle with her.

"Oh, she decided not to continue with Girl Scouts. She has a lot of other things she needs to do. She is a straight-A student, you know," my mother said to our neighbor. I would hear my mother tell people calmly and almost proudly that I had made a decision not to continue with Girl Scouts. My mother always had a cheery tone of voice when she would discuss her wonderful family at bridge club, church, or school. Everything was always wonderful, or so she told her friends. Who knows? Maybe she really believed what she said. I was confused. My experience of things at home was not as my mother described it to other people. I can remember thinking I must be wrong or confused about what was happening at home. I learned not to trust my perceptions.

We went to school and church with our neighbors. Our neighbors were all from a similar background. I grew up in a very ethnic city, but all ethnic groups were segregated at that time. The Greeks, the Poles, Italians, Lithuanians each had their own section of the city in which they lived. It wasn't exclusionary, or we didn't think so. We all lived with our own kind. That contributed to the predictability of our lives. I can't judge whether it was a good thing. It was just that way. All I can say is that later, as an adult, when I lived in a large ethnically mixed city, life could be very stressful. We didn't know what to expect from each other and other people did not behave in a manner I was used to. The stress was, at times, exhausting. Every daily interaction had to be negotiated and renegotiated just like in my marriages.

"She's here," I heard one of the other mothers whisper to my mother. All of the mothers were seated at a couple of tables talking together. They all turned their heads to look in the direction of the entrance. We were all spending the day at the community swim club. That is what we did in the summers. There were no day camps and very few sleep-away camps. Usually those were too expensive to attend anyway. The woman they were all staring at didn't come and sit at the table with all the other mothers. She sat on the other side of the pool with her two children—in the teenager section. I noticed that no one talked to her at all during the time she was there. The women never discussed why she didn't sit with them, at least in my presence. I was confused. These same women who wouldn't acknowledge her were so supportive and caring toward each other. I didn't understand how they could be so unkind to this woman. I picked up on the reason over time. She was divorced. There was no such thing as divorces in the fifties and sixties. To put it mildly, differences were not appreciated in the fifties and sixties. Conformity, not compassion, was the buzzword although no one would ever overtly admit that. I was terrified to be different, at least on the outside. If you are different or make mistakes (like a divorce), you are not shown kindness or compassion, or so I learned. Compassion had its limits. It was reserved for people who followed the rules (often unwritten) and for needy people that you learned about at church. But really the needy people received pity, not compassion.

Family vacations were typically road trips. Our family vacations consisted of visits by car to all the historical spots within several days driving distance of where we lived. We had three channels on TV. Television went off the air at ten pm. Cartoons were only aired on Saturday mornings. Tampons and ED were not advertised on TV. Black people did not appear in TV commercials until much later. Birthdays were celebrated by inviting the neighborhood kids over for cake and ice cream. Gifts were a rarity. We played sports or hung out with the other kids in the neighborhood. Sex was a total mystery and was never ever mentioned. In my house you couldn't even say the word "sex." Only the routine events of the day were ever discussed. They were typically discussed at the nightly dinner table.

Families on TV behaved perfectly. They always got along. They always behaved nicely. They never argued or fought with each other or their friends. Any mistakes they made were minor and easily fixed. We were expected to be like these families. Of course, we were doomed to failure. Now, on TV, we primarily see people that behave abominably. I think it has lowered the standards for behavior in our own everyday life. I hope we can find a middle ground. As a child and young adult, I so admired the people on TV because they didn't have many emotions or they were able to remain calm and control their emotions at all times. I tried very hard to be like them. There had to be something wrong with me since I had to struggle so to control my emotions.

"Girls, are you dressed yet?" my mother shouted up the stairs. My sister and I had already managed to put on our frilly new dresses, lace ankle socks, and patent leather shoes. We had helped each other with buttons and buckles. We were squealing with delight.

"We're coming," we shouted down. We were still putting on our hats with the ribbons streaming down. It was such an exciting time! We weren't going to Sunday school this day. We were too young to take communion, but since it was Easter, we were going to stay in the church with our parents for the entire service! We raced down the stairs. My mother carefully inspected us. My father and brother were dressed in suits and ties. My mother had on a new dress with a matching hat. My mother, sister, and I wore white gloves.

When we arrived at the church, my parents greeted everyone in the narthex. As soon as we entered the sanctuary, we were admonished to be very quiet. There was a beautiful stained glass window in the front of the church. In the middle of that window was a huge cross. The sun was streaming through that window filling the sanctuary with light and warmth. Beautiful hymns were being played on the organ. The choir members were dressed in their robes and waiting in the narthex for their procession into the sanctuary. The minister was dressed in his black vestments with a purple sash. As we walked closer to the front of the church I saw many of my schoolmates sitting with their parents and siblings and sometimes grandparents. We weren't allowed to talk to each other. They too were dressed in frilly, lacy dresses, and bonnets. The boys were in suits and ties. The ushers were setting up extra chairs around the sanctuary. The church would be overflowing. After we sat down, the minister and choir proceeded up the aisle singing "Jesus Christ is risen today… Alleluia!" As they entered the sanctuary we all rose and joined them in singing that hymn.

My sister and I felt a bit wilted by the end of the service. After the service, our parents visited with our friends, neighbors, parents of our schoolmates. We got to play with our friends.

"Be careful with your new dress and shoes," my mother scolded us. We didn't stay too long at church. We had to drive to our grandparents' house which was about an hour away to spend the holiday with my aunt, uncle, and cousins. We did that almost every year. We would all sit down together to eat a wonderful Easter dinner of roast lamb my grandmother had prepared. Then we could change clothes and play with our cousins while our mother, aunt, and grandmother cleaned up the kitchen.

Religion, or at least church, was an integral part of my childhood. It was one of the foundations of our community. Our time at church was both religious and social. My Sunday school class was made up primarily of my classmates from school and my teacher was almost always the mother of one of my friends. It was an outing—a break from the monotony of being at home. We didn't have all the options for recreation the children do now. I have wonderful memories of the church of my childhood although that is not where my faith in God was born. But, perhaps the seeds were planted there.

In the summer we all went to Bible school. It is hard to imagine in these current times, but we looked forward to those two weeks. Bible school was our break from the monotony of playing with the neighborhood kids. Neighborhood activities were fun, but we wanted some variety. Many of my schoolmates attended Bible school along with me. My mother and the mothers of my classmates were the teachers. We had arts and crafts. We learned stories from the Bible like we did in Sunday school. We had some recreation time together. The world felt safe and comfortable.

"Are we going to get to go the first day—Friday night?" I asked my mother. "Can we go on Saturday as well? Can we play all the games? Can we buy something?" I continued to pester her. I was asking about the Fall Festival at the church, which was going to take place in a couple of weeks. My sister and I were very excited. It was an annual event. My mother was usually one of the organizers of that event. It took months to arrange and coordinate everything. Volunteers had to be procured and scheduled to man the many the booths and cook the dinner. The booths had to be set up by the fathers on the weekends or evenings. White elephant items had to be procured, tagged, and displayed for sale. We played games and won prizes. My favorite game was throwing a bean bag into a backboard one of the fathers had made and painted. There was great food. We always had a dinner but there were snacks as well. I can still smell the sautéed mushrooms that were being prepared in electric skillets at one of the booths. As I think back to the church festivals and other church events, I am overcome with a feeling of warmth and comfort.

As I matured, I remained involved in the church. I taught Sunday school. I participated in the high school youth group. I attended church summer camp for two weeks. I wasn't sure if I was going to be able to do that. It was an expensive camp and I overheard my parents discussing if they could afford it. In the end, they made some financial sacrifices because they thought it was important for me to attend. What a thrill!

Our childhood days and years had a distinct rhythm to them. The sameness of our daily events and the uniformity of our lives were comforting. It connected us into a community. But in that world of intense physical connectedness, I felt emotionally disconnected and isolated. The predictable rhythm of the days, years and events served as an anchor and also as a prison. The rhythm and sameness of our lives was our savior and a source of our comfort but also of pain. There was a script or formula we were to follow if we wanted to have the happy lives we lived as children. In fact, we were guaranteed that if we followed the script we would have a good life. That happened for some of us, but it failed miserably to prepare others for the world some of us would inhabit as adults, that is, worlds that deviated drastically from the script. I had no idea how far my life would deviate from the script and what a sense of failure that deviation would create.

It woke me up—the screaming. I looked at the clock on my nightstand. It was two o'clock in the morning. I could hear my parents screaming at each other. In all of my sixteen years, I had never heard them even raise their voices at each other. I listened for a while. They were saying something about my younger sister and hospital. I was afraid. I pulled the covers up over my head waiting for this to be over. More time passed and the screaming continued. I don't know why, but I ventured out to the living room. As I passed my sister's room I didn't hear anything and the door was closed tightly. Both of my parents were in their pajamas standing in the middle of the living room. My sister was nowhere in sight. My mother was crying—not uncontrollable sobs, she just had tears in her eyes. I had never seen that before or since.

My father was shrieking, "I am sick to death of her. I don't care what happens to her. Just let her die!" He stormed out of the living room into the bedroom and slammed the door. Between the stomping and the door slamming the whole house shook. I had quietly taken a seat in one of the chairs in the corner of the living room.

My mother didn't say a word to me or even look at me. She got up and went to the kitchen to make a phone call. "Can you send an ambulance to 642 Mulberry Lane right away? My daughter has swallowed an entire bottle of some type of pills—aspirin, I think."

I was dumbfounded. Why had she done it? Had there been warning signs? My sister was and always had been, you know, (it was whispered) "emotional." My parents in their typical fashion explained away her behavior—behavior she exhibited her entire life – as a phase, a stage. As a last resort they would explain that she was just an emotional person. Being an emotional person in the world of my childhood was akin to having a terrible disease. Emotional persons were the lepers of the that world. There wasn't much worse you could say about a person back then. I did occasionally hear some veiled expressions of sympathy expressed to my parents regarding my sister being emotional. Things were whispered or looks were given as if her condition was a curse from God. My parents had a real ability to ignore or explain away abnormal behavior. They never wanted to deal with a problem head on. Those things were never discussed. My sister was just that way, or so my parents believed. They hoped she would grow out of it. She never did.

I never heard my mother mention or even allude to my sister's attempted suicide. My sister and I talked about it a little bit when she came home from the psychiatric hospital. But except as between the two of us, my sister's behavior and this episode were another secret we carried around with us like the secret of my mother's verbal abuse. To this day, almost forty years later, no one in our family has ever even tried to discuss the episode. After this many years, that is probably best.

I passed through my childhood with a constant feeling in the pit of my stomach like something bad was going to happen. I was always anxious, tense, and afraid. I was terrified I would do something wrong. My emotions raged out of control but I never let on how I was feeling. I was able to control them for the most part. To the world and my parents my inner life appeared as calm and predictable and controlled as our outer life. We children intuitively knew never to discuss the inner workings of our family with anyone. To this day I have not discussed any of this with anyone not even my sister. Well that is not exactly true I may have told my therapist, I don't really recall.

Yes, I learned in my childhood that there are good and bad feelings. Bad feelings or problems were simply swept under the rug. My family didn't discuss or express those, only mundane, pleasant things, the banalities of life. If we did discuss anything more, we would be labeled "emotional" like my sister, which was equivalent to being defective. I never heard my parents express compassion for my sister recognizing that perhaps she was in a lot of emotional pain. She saw a psychiatrist for a while so he could fix her. She was simply an embarrassment because she wouldn't control herself. She acted out constantly, got bad grades, and engaged in other unacceptable behavior. People showed pity toward my parents and my sister, but pity is not compassion. Pity includes a great deal of judgment whereas compassion is judgment free.

I felt as if I had been kicked in the stomach when I watched the movie *Ordinary People* as a young adult. It was perhaps the scariest movie I have seen. I have never been able to watch it again. It expressed the reality of my childhood better than I can. When I saw it, it stirred up all the feelings of emptiness, loneliness and fear of my childhood—the black hole opened up. I can remember when I tried to tell my ex-husband, David, about how it made me feel, he told me I was stupid and walked away.

I remember once, as a child, hearing a clanking like the sound of something metal striking an object. I turned to look at my father. My father was seated at the head of the dinner table. But he wasn't serving the dinner plates to each person as was his custom. Instead, his face contorted with rage, he was throwing pieces of silverware in the direction of my mother although I don't know that he was aiming for her. I froze.

I heard a few more clanking sounds and then my father stormed off to his bedroom, slamming the door behind him.

"Let's eat," my mother said cheerfully without batting an eye. "The food is getting cold." My mother didn't smile much, but she had a smile plastered on her face as she said this. My brother, sister, and I were all seated in our respective places at the dinner table. My mother went around to the head of the table and began serving the plates. We ate our dinner in silence. Fortunately, my father hadn't hit anyone. My father never emerged from his room that night. He was already at work when we left for school the next morning. Everything was back to normal the next night at the dinner table.

My dad was a very kind and gentle man who also had a fierce temper that very rarely flared up. He was interested in you and what you were doing as long as it was something he was interested in. That pretty much limited the sphere of interaction with him to books and reading. Anytime he wanted to go somewhere or do something, even if I was not interested in it, I went with him. When he wanted to talk to me, I was always available. This was true even as a teenager and into adulthood. I am not complaining, mind you. I learned a lot and I acquired a lifelong interest in books, reading, history, etc. as a result of my relationship with my dad. I have good memories and good feelings when I think of my dad. I love my father. He was one of the bright spots in an otherwise bleak childhood.

As a child I felt like I had to take care of my dad and my sister. On many occasions I talked my sister out of running away from home. I can remember sitting on the stairs of our small house convincing her to stay. I have no idea where my parents were. My mom had simply walked away when my sister announced she was running away. I had to protect them from my mother. I had to be my dad's and sister's emotional support, or so I thought.

I used to do my homework at the dining room table after my mother had cleared away the dirty dinner dishes. My dad was usually sitting in the living room in his favorite chair reading a book. Once my mother cleaned up the kitchen she would join him in the living room. She loved to knit, work on crossword puzzles and play cards—solitaire primarily.

My sister was often watching TV downstairs although we got so few channels I can't imagine what she could find to see. I think my brother usually did his homework in his room.

"I have a presbytery meeting tomorrow morning. We are going to discuss World Day of Prayer. The Fall Festival is rapidly approaching. We have a meeting Wednesday to plan that event. Martha Harris and I are going to recruit some other women to handle individual booths. We are planning to have booths of baked goods, games, crafts, and a sales booth for some white elephant items. We have been asking the congregation to drop off donations for the white elephant sales at the church," my mother rattled off.

"Do people really want to buy other people's junk?" my dad asked. My mother sighed.

"How were things at the office today?" my mother asked.

"Well, the production is up at the forge. We have some new orders that have been recently placed. The union contract is up for renewal but we have a very good relationship with the members so I don't foresee any problems," my dad replied. The sound of their voices in the background was very comforting as I turned back to my homework.

"We can't afford it. I won't fill out the financial aid application. Those colleges think parents should contribute huge amounts of money. It is ridiculous. We can't contribute anywhere near the amount they will want from us," my father said. I had worked incredibly hard to have the credentials to be admitted to an Ivy League or similar university. Now my father refused to allow me to apply. This was one of my first huge disappointments in life. I had the sophomoric notion that God could make this happen if He wanted to. In those days my faith in God was rather immature and I was angry at God. Other kids from my high school were accepted and attended the schools I wanted to go to. Their credentials were not always as good as mine.

"Brad, my brother, is attending a very expensive university away from home. Why can't I do the same?" I complained to my father.

"He will have to support a family," my father said to explain why my brother got to attend the university of his choice and I didn't. I never got the message, which I understand some of my peers did, that a woman could be anything she wanted to be. I felt alienated from the world in which I had grown up and by implication that included God. I was depressed. I lived at home and attended college. That is what my parents could afford. I wouldn't give God much thought again, if any, for at least eighteen years.

My mother apparently had issues with contributing anything to my education. "Dad, Mother refuses to put the money I need for college into my bank account. I can't even buy any food until she does that. I have been asking her for several weeks. Now she just hangs up on me when I call," I said as I started to cry.

"Now dear…," my dad said. He always said the same things. I was imaging it. My mother had been busy and was going to do it right away. I could wait a little longer. My father never did realize how badly my mother treated my sister and me. I am not sure why I even talked to him about it on this particular occasion. Usually I just muscled through it. I'm not sure why I asked my mother about the money. I learned long ago not to ask her for things. If I asked for something I would be sure I wouldn't get it or it wouldn't happen. You would think I would have learned that lesson well by the time I was in college.

My dad had an uncanny ability to live in a world of his own imaging, and he never imagined my mother acted this way. He was oblivious to how she treated us and he remained oblivious until sadly, at the end of their life together, he became the recipient of her behavior. I was sorry he had to experience that. I would rather he remained oblivious.

"When you graduate from college, you are on your own. Don't ask us for anything else," my mother constantly told me. I worked very hard to comply with that request. I didn't ask for or receive any financial assistance when I attended law school. My father's comment when I told him I was going to attend law school was that I should stay home with my children.

"Your grandfather has passed away," my mother told me. I was in my first year of college. I was devastated. He was the only outwardly loving, fun member of our family. He always made me laugh and feel happy. Everyone he met loved him. It is funny, but my oldest son resembles him a little in character and interestingly is named after him.

By today's standards, he did not live long enough. He was only seventy-three. Just that past summer I had stayed with my grandparents and helped out for a few weeks. I felt so connected to him while I was there. He even told me some things about his life I doubt he had shared with anyone else in the family. I don't know that I was that special to him. I was just physically present when he knew he was dying.

"Janet," my grandmother called out desperately to my mother. "I can't believe it. I just can't believe your father is gone." My grandmother started to cry and reached out to hug my mother. It had only been a week since my grandfather's funeral. My grandmother was able to catch herself before she fell. You see, my mother had turned her back on my grandmother and simply walked away.

"He's gone, Mother," is all my mother said as she left the room. My mother always called my grandmother "Mother."

My grandmother got a hold of herself in our true family fashion. I never saw my grandmother cry or grieve again. I never saw my mother comfort her mother or even acknowledge her grief. I never saw my mother grieve either. She never shed a tear that I saw. By her own account my mother adored my grandfather. She was, by all accounts, a daddy's girl. How could my mother be so heartless to her mother?

I never saw either of my parents cry or grieve when any of their parents died. Did they love their parents? I know my mother claimed to love my grandfather very much. "Do you love me?" I asked each of my parents on a very rare occasion.

"That is a silly question," each of them responded. Was it?

I hated my mother for most of my life. Maybe hate is too strong a word, but I definitely did not like her. I thought she was a terrible mother and person. I could never understand how people in the community could speak so highly of her and with great affection.

From my mother, I had learned to judge, criticize, blame, condemn and avoid those who had problems or were going through really difficult times. I avoided those who did not conform to the way of life I thought everyone should live. I learned to pity the less fortunate, but that is looking down on someone because they are having trouble. We would help the less fortunate through community service with the church. Pity is not showing compassion. I learned those lessons from my childhood so well. Now I would have to unlearn them if I wanted to make peace with myself, my life, and my choices and to connect with others.

But the lessons my mother taught me went deep. Certainly I didn't want to share any of my problems with others because they would judge and criticize me. It was a barrier I think I still run into on some level. So for most of my life, I felt totally alone and isolated because I could only share the good parts of my life and myself with others. I had to create a façade of managing everything well without any help.

Asking for help would make me appear weak and needy. I needed to appear strong and in control at all times if I was to avoid being pitied or worse. But that was all a façade. What it was really is that I didn't know how, and I was afraid to ask for help. It was only when my world began to unravel with my first husband that I got my first inkling of the power of compassion. Still I don't think I really recognized the power of compassion at that time. It certainly felt nice when someone took the time to pay attention to me and even offer help, but it was not a part of my daily life. Once the crisis passed, the compassion went with it. Thus, as I was just learning about the magic that comes with compassion, I misread it. I associated compassion only with crises. I would need to go through more trials and tribulations before I really learned to show compassion toward others and myself as a way of life. I was still blind to the magic of compassion.

When my therapist asked me to open the floodgates and pour out all the muck that had built up around my parents and mother, I didn't like it. But I knew it was necessary to heal all that heartache if I was going to make peace with my life and find a way of living that did not include the lessons of my childhood like judgment, criticism, failure, and pity. I didn't realize it then, but as I healed and focused on the good parts of my life, I began to see that they all involved compassion, and as my journey towards living with compassion continued, I was grateful that I was no longer carrying all that extra baggage.

CHAPTER FOUR

The First Inkling of Self-Compassion

A<small>FTER MY FIRST DIVORCE, I WAS ANGRY AND BITTER. C</small>OMPASSION was, for the most part, not present in my everyday life. I was angry at the world because other peoples' lives were not as difficult as mine. I felt my life was a constant emotional and financial struggle to survive. The recent events of the divorce, domestic violence, and at the pressure of being a single mom without any support took a toll on me.

Three innocent children were left in the sole care of an emotionally distraught and physically exhausted mother. I soldiered on with the daily demands of living, but the rage and hurt were vented against the people who needed me the most and whom I loved the most—my children.

Everything was a crisis in those days. I was exhausted all the time. I was overwhelmed by the demands of daily living. Work was stressful. It was a constant battle to find affordable childcare for three young children. I was reeling from receiving threats and being harassed by the children's father. The children were acting out and not doing well at school. The house was a mess all the time. The laundry was always piled high. We lived paycheck to paycheck. I would rush home from the office, cook dinner, and help a little with homework, get the younger two bathed and in bed, wash the dinner dishes, and fall into bed exhausted hopefully by nine-thirty p.m. Then I would start everything over again the next day at six-thirty a.m. On the weekends we went to the grocery where some weeks we had only twenty-five dollars for groceries. I was able to take the children on one fun outing each week. We usually went to a park or other free venue to try to have some fun. This is the environment in which my children spent their early, formative years.

"Mom, Ellen is crying again," Jessica told me. It wasn't like I didn't know. I had just walked in the door from the office. It was about six-thirty p.m. I saw Ellen sitting in the hallway that connected the main part of the small house to the bedrooms. She was hugging her stuffed animal and sobbing. "Oh, my God," I thought to myself. Another night of listening to her constant sobbing. I was exhausted already from a stressful day at the office. I still had to cook dinner, clean up the kitchen, monitor homework, bathe the kids, and then collapse into bed.

"Ellen, stop crying. There is nothing wrong with you!" I said sternly as I walked past her on my way to the kitchen. I didn't offer her any comfort.

"Ellen, come eat your dinner," I said sternly a little bit later. She didn't move. Finally, I went to her, stroked her head and said matter-of-factly, "I love you. Everything will be all right. Come have some dinner now."

She came and ate some dinner still crying a bit. In fact, Ellen continued to cry for the rest of the evening. She had been doing that every evening for several months—ever since her father had moved out of the house. As soon as I walked through the door, she would start to cry. Listening to a child cry just frays one's nerves. I was no exception and my nerves were already severely frayed. I was desperate to get her to stop. I finally coaxed her into my bed about eight-thirty p.m. She was exhausted and quickly fell asleep. I knew this was only a brief reprieve as it would all start again the next night as soon as I walked through the door. This went on for months. I was desperate to get her to stop. One night I sat down next to Ellen in the hallway and pretended to cry. The funny thing is that real tears came down my cheeks. We cried together for several nights. After that Ellen just stopped sitting in the hallway and crying. If only I had thought to do that sooner.

Usually the children were at the front door to greet me when I came home from the office, and they would be jostling each other to try to get my attention. Ellen would join them after she stopped her months of crying.

"Mom, I need help with my homework," Jessica would say.

"Mom, Samuel hit me," Ellen would complain.

"Mom, the sitter was mean to me today," Samuel would say woefully.

They would all end up shouting at me as each of them tried to get my attention. I would squeeze past them giving each a perfunctory hello and a hug before I rushed to the kitchen to prepare dinner. I know they each wanted some one-on-one time with me, but it would have to wait until after dinner. They were all overwrought with hunger by the time I arrived home. All three of them would continue to talk to me at the same time as I prepared dinner. I would try to get them to take turns but it was pretty impossible.

"How could you have lost your glasses?" I screamed at five-year-old Samuel. "I can't afford to buy you another pair right now!" I shrieked. I continued ranting and raving—venting my frustration at poor little Samuel for a while longer. Every extra expenditure was a huge crisis in those days. I can't really remember what Samuel said or did, if anything. I'm sure he was used to me, by that time, ranting and raving about just about everything that happened.

During the unraveling of my first marriage and afterwards, I couldn't wait to get out of the office at lunchtime so I could go for a drive. I would race to my car and drive into a quiet residential neighborhood not far from the office. I would park my car, put my head down on the steering wheel of the car and sob for my entire one-hour lunch break. I would clean my face up, or so I hoped, and go back to the office. Thankfully the people at the office were gracious enough not to ask me what had happened. I think they instinctively knew I couldn't handle their questions. They were quietly compassionate.

"What do you mean, you can't count money?" I asked Jessica. "It is simple. Here is how you do it," I impatiently said in a raised voice. A five minute, hostile demonstration ensued after which I left to clean up the kitchen after dinner. Jessica struggled with that issue and others for quite a while. She didn't ask me again for any help with her homework. Of course my message to Jessica was that she was stupid even though I don't think I ever said that word. She wasn't stupid. The problem was me. I didn't have the patience to help her, and I didn't recognize that all I needed to do what take a deep breath, take an extra five minutes to help her figure out part of it, and she would get it. I was parenting as I had been parented.

I have also come to know that beating myself up about it doesn't help me—or Jessica. The real lesson is being able to recognize when someone needs a small moment of compassion—showing some care and helping. Showing compassion really doesn't take much time—certainly less time than berating her took.

I didn't know how to tell people what was going on, how hard things were or that I needed help. I felt people whispered about my children, i.e. that they were problem children. Of course they were. People judged you as a single mother. You were a failure because you couldn't make you marriage work. They judged you as a lousy mother because your children misbehaved. I responded to those attitudes by being defensive and abrasive. I take some responsibility for these attitudes because perhaps if I had shared with people what was going on they would have been more compassionate. Who knows because I never tried. I was afraid they would reject me and the children even more if I shared even some parts of my life with them. I was keeping secrets as I had learned to do so well as a child. To be honest, if someone had told me a story like mine, I'm not sure how I would have reacted. I doubt at this point in my life that I would have offered much compassion. I might have been sympathetic, but I think I would have judged, condemned and avoided the person. In part it is through our own difficult experiences that we learn to be compassionate.

"Samuel has been missing on his bike for several hours," the after-school babysitter told me over the phone. He was five years old at the time. I left the office in a panic and drove around our neighborhood. I found Samuel riding his bike with some older boys in the desert. This wasn't the first or last time I would receive that phone call. Changing sitters was not much use. There were not many childcare options in those days, and I couldn't afford daycare for three children.

Sometimes I could find a sitter who was affordable, reliable, and cooked dinner, but that was the exception, and they didn't last long. Sylvia was one of those, but about a week after she started she wanted a dollar-an-hour raise. I couldn't afford that, so she left. Sitters came and went on a regular basis. My children were not the easiest to take care of. Samuel and Ellen weren't keen on following rules, to put it mildly.

"I quit," the babysitter told me as soon as I walked in the door from the office. "Samuel is impossible. He doesn't follow any rules. He is impossible to control. He does what he wants, when he wants. He took off on his bike again today and was gone for three hours. I was afraid to call you again," she said in exasperation. I couldn't argue with her because it was all so true. This was the third sitter that had quit in about four months. As if finding them was not difficult enough—keeping them was even harder. I hoped she would agree to stay until I could find someone else.

Martha was the receptionist at the office and my compassionate friend. We met at the office. She started at the office around the time I did. We came from totally different backgrounds. Martha was one of thirteen children. She barely finished high school. I had graduated from law school. Her husband, Manny, worked as an auto mechanic. Martha knew I was struggling financially, and she offered to have Manny fix my car. He would fix my car for the cost of the parts and a six pack of beer. The children and I would spend the day at their house which was not in the best part of town. Martha would fix us fabulous meals. She and Manny opened their hearts and their home to us. My children would play with their six children. Martha and Manny had their own financial struggles, yet they shared what they had with us. They really could have used the money I should have paid to have my car fixed. Have you noticed that it is often the people who have the least to share who share the most? Their compassion brings tears to my eyes still. We have remained connected all these many years even though life and great distances have separated us from each other. When we do get together, it is as if the years just melt away. Compassion heals and connects us. Their compassion helped healed my anger and hurt. Someone cared. Someone helped. I didn't even have to ask most of the time. She just often sensed what I needed.

Compassion creates strong and lasting bonds. Most people would not see Manny and Martha as compassionate people because of where they come from, where they live, and how they look. That is their loss.

Martha came running into my office. "The school is calling about Samuel," she said worriedly and, as always, without judgment. I picked up the phone.

"This is Dr. Howard. I am the school psychologist at Remington Elementary School. We tested Samuel in preparation for kindergarten. He has a learning disability and we recommend he be placed in a special education class for a year before hopefully matriculating to a regular kindergarten class." I left the office in tears and drove home.

"Ma'am, this is the police department. We have your son, Samuel, here at the convenience store. He and some other boys tried to steal some chewing gum." Samuel was about six years or seven years old at the time. I guess this is one of the places he would ride to on his bike when he would disappear. The officer was great. He talked to Samuel. I don't know if it sunk in or not. Samuel was totally out of control, so I doubt it.

I took Samuel's bike to the office and stored it there. He had already lost most, if not all, of his toys as consequences for his bad behavior.

"I don't care," was all he would say when I would threaten or impose another consequence. For oh-so-many good reasons I needed him to follow the basic rules. I tried all kinds of discipline tactics, but nothing seemed to work.

"Samuel, pack a suitcase, and get in the car. You have to find someplace else to live," I said finally.

"Where are you going?" Jessica asked Samuel.

"Mom is giving me away," Samuel replied very matter-of-factly. After we got in the car, I started to drive around our neighborhood.

"Samuel, you have to find another place to live unless you can agree to follow the rules," I said sternly. "Will you follow the rules?" I asked. Samuel was silent. I stopped the car. "This kid is going to call my bluff," I remember thinking to myself. He is the most stubborn kid on the planet. "Get out and go knock on one of these doors, and ask if you can live there," I said. Samuel didn't move. "Do you want to come home and follow the rules?" I asked hopefully. Again Samuel was silent. He got out of the car and stood at the corner holding his little suitcase. My heart sank. It was getting dark. "Do you want to go home with me?" I asked. Samuel was silent.

"Okay, I am leaving now," I said. I drove away and around the block. My heart was racing. What was I going to do? I waited what seemed like an eternity and then I drove back to where I had left him. He was standing in the exact same spot on the corner, still clutching his little suitcase. I opened the passenger door. "Do you want to come home and follow the rules?" I asked.

Samuel nodded his head, "Yes." He got into the car. Samuel's behavior improved somewhat after that. At least I was able to keep a babysitter for longer than a month or two. It definitely wasn't the best way to handle it, but I was desperate. I couldn't work unless I had a babysitter. I couldn't keep a babysitter unless Samuel behaved. Samuel's refusal to follow even the most basic rules could result in him getting hurt or worse.

Jessica refused to go to the sitter's house which was fortunately just next door. She went home by herself after school. She was in third grade! She was required to call me at the office as soon as she arrived home.

"Jessica, you didn't call me today when you got home from school," I said when she answered the phone. "I was really worried."

"Sorry, Mom, I forgot," Jessica replied.

"Don't do that again," I demanded. "Are you doing your homework? How much do you have?" I grilled her.

"You have a call," I heard Margie say over the office intercom.

"I have to go now. Please start your homework, and I will call you a little later," I said to Jessica. I was too busy to call later that day. I hoped she knew she could call me if she had a problem or question. It was a constant worry every day.

"Let's go over your homework," I said as I started to clear the table.

"Mom, we have a project due next week, and I need to buy some things at the store in the next day or two so I can get started," Jessica said.

"Mom, I have a play at school next week. Can you get my costume tonight?" Ellen said.

"I have a note from my teacher," said Samuel as pushed a piece of crumpled paper in my hand and skulked away to his room.

"Well, let's talk while I clean up the kitchen and you do your homework," I replied. Of course, in reality, I was rarely that composed or even patient. I know there was an edge to my voice all the time—anger and impatience.

"Has everyone taken their bath?" I shouted from the kitchen. "Has everyone finished their homework?" I shouted a few minutes later. "It is bedtime," I shouted. Homework was usually done by eight or eight thirty. If I was lucky the kitchen was cleaned up by nine or nine thirty. Sometimes I had to pack lunches depending on the budget that week. I couldn't afford to pay for school lunches for two and later three children every day of the month.

There were two science fair projects to be completed at the same time! Good heavens, how could I find the time and money to do that? It seemed like a lost cause anyway. My children couldn't compete with the other children in their classes. All of those children had two parents with a lot more time and financial resources than I did. Things were getting better, but we still didn't have much extra money. Energy to find a better job just didn't exist. My energy was focused on keeping the one that I had. I couldn't let anyone see any of the stress or problems at the office—not if I wanted to keep my job. Sure, some of it showed, but I was always at the office, and I had the requisite number of billable hours. I worked like a maniac when I was there. Work was actually my salvation. I could forget about everything else while I was working, for the most part. The little vacation I had I would use to go on field trips with the kids and attend their school programs during the day. I know they felt different because they didn't have a dad.

It was as if I was outside my body hearing myself shrieking at Jessica. I don't remember exactly what I said. Some voice in my head was able to reach me through the rage. "You are just like your mother," I heard the voice say. I stopped in mid-sentence. I can remember that moment with Jessica like it just happened yesterday. I was standing in the hallway of our little house in the desert. Oh my God, how did I get here? How did I become my mother? I so wanted to give my children something better!

That realization propelled me to make time again to see Dr. M., the psychologist who had helped me before. You see, part of the problem was that I knew what a bad parent looked like, but I had no idea what a good parent looked like. I couldn't change the stress I was under, but I needed to cope with it better for the sake of my children. I was a terrible parent for a long time, and I felt guilty and terrible about myself because of it. Later in my life I would learn to practice some self-compassion and forgive myself.

At home I had always made it my main focus to provide physical stability for the kids like nightly family dinners, getting homework done, family outings, and outings with some friends on the weekends. Of course that was all peppered with an occasional verbal bashing. I was able to talk a little bit about my struggles with the children with the office manager at work. She was a bit shocked by it all but she was also compassionate. Her husband was a teacher and he suggested a few books for me to read. Those books helped me tremendously. One suggested spending time each night with each child. I started devoting just ten to fifteen minutes every night to each of the children individually. They would get into bed and I would come into their room. I would sit on the edge of their bed and just ask them about their day, etc. We called these sessions our "talking tos." That may have one of the best things I ever did as a parent. I wished then and now I had more energy for those talking tos. Still in spite of my lack of time and energy and sometimes patience, the children loved their one-on-one time with me. Some twenty years later, they still talk about it reverently.

"Jessica, your grades have dropped. What is going on?" I asked her. She was in fourth grade at the time. She looked at me strangely and shrugged her shoulders. I could tell I wasn't going to find out what was going on from Jessica. I called her teacher and scheduled a conference. The teacher was kind enough to come to school early to meet me so that I could get to the office on time. I arrived at school around seven forty-five a.m. The teacher was in the classroom. We chatted a little bit about Jessica's school work. I detected a little hostility, but I was awfully tired and stressed out in those days, so I thought I was imagining it.

"Jessica is not doing as well as she did last year or even earlier this year, and she doesn't want to come to school lately. Is there something going on with the other kids that I should know about?" I asked.

"No," was the response.

"Do you have any idea what may be causing this change?" I continued to probe the teacher.

"No," she responded again.

I asked, "Where does Jessica sit?" I have no idea why I asked that question. The teacher pointed out the location of Jessica's desk. It was located in the very last row in the far corner of the classroom. It was the desk that was furthest away from the teacher and the chalkboard. My facial expression must have reflected my surprise.

Somewhat sheepishly the teacher explained, "I moved her there a few weeks ago."

"Why is she sitting there if she is having problems?" I asked. "Shouldn't she be in the front of the room?" The teacher had stopped looking at me at this point in the conversation. I pressed the issue. "Why isn't Jessica sitting in the front of the classroom?" I really can't remember exactly what the teacher said. I just remember that it made no sense and seemed to be a perfectly ridiculous explanation. I trusted my instincts, for once, and said in a firm voice, "I will expect her to be moved to the front of the room right away." There was no verbal response although I did receive a brief look of contempt. "I hope I don't have to go to the principal about this," I said as I got up and left.

Jessica was moved to the front of the room. She started to enjoy going to school again and her grades improved. Was I imagining the teacher's hostility and contempt? Was I imagining that the poor treatment was a result of my status as a divorced woman and single mother? Maybe. I tended to doubt myself and my perceptions in those days. I still do. Things certainly changed for the better for Jessica after my talk with her teacher. Maybe by confronting her about her treatment of Jessica, she realized what she was doing. Maybe she just wasn't aware of what she was doing. I hope that was the case.

The school Jessica attended was located in a wealthy suburban area which was primarily populated by married couples in traditional households.

Fortunately for us, and unfortunately for them, it encompassed more than just those types of families. There were other similar incidents after this one. Eventually I learned to intercede before the situation got really bad, or maybe I just stopped giving the teachers the benefit of the doubt. I am a slow learner. My children say I am bit naive. Maybe so. I wish I had learned that lesson sooner. My children may have been spared some pain and humiliation. Must everyone who is different pay a price? Children of divorce may not any longer be considered different and subjected to such treatment but others are.

I was pretty tough in those days, or at least I thought I was. I certainly had to go outside the parameters of the traditional female role in order to survive and take care of my children. That required engaging in some traditional male behaviors such as direct confrontations with others. That created some anxiety for me at first but like most things in life I got used to it.

I knocked on my neighbor's door. They lived directly across the street from us. Samuel was about five or six years old at the time. Samuel's Big Wheel had been broken by an older child in the neighborhood. Jessica had seen this neighbor's son, who was in fifth grade, riding the Big Wheel. Jessica had also told me that this boy teased and picked on Samuel at the bus stop and on the school bus. So I found myself at my neighbor's door. I figured that the father would be upset his son was engaging in this behavior. I wasn't angry when I knocked. The father answered the door.

"I would like to talk to you about some problems at the bus stop. I believe your son is teasing my son at the bus stop and on the school bus."

Before I could say any more the father shouted, "You are a stupid b****, and your kid is an idiot!"

I jumped right into the fray. "Well, your son broke my son's Big Wheel!"

"Get the hell out of here!" he said as he started to slam the door in my face.

"I know now why he is the way he is. He better not touch my son again!" I shouted back.

Every morning when I went to get in my car to go to work, this neighbor would come out of his house and stare at me menacingly. This went on for a few weeks. The dad was just a crazy person, but I also think it had something to do with the fact that I was an easy target as a single mom. He was also a little threatened by me. I was experiencing the same thing in the work environment during this time. Things didn't improve at the bus stop until I took direct action. "If you touch my son again, I will find you and beat you up," I told the kid one day as he gave me the finger at the bus stop. I wasn't proud of myself for threatening a fifth grader, but I didn't know what else to do. The bullying stopped after that. I guess the kid thought I looked angry or crazy enough to actually follow through on my threat. In those days I think he might have been right.

Compassion is a funny thing. It is not really something we can ask for. It starts with the giver. Something about another's situation triggers a feeling of wanting to help to alleviate the other's suffering or situation. I believe we sense when others are struggling. Typically, when someone is in the throes of a difficult time, they don't have the wherewithal to reach out to others. They are immersed in dealing with their own situation—difficult circumstances. They are most likely embarrassed and ashamed. Maybe they are feeling judged or are angry at themselves and the world.

I know I had all of these feelings and more during this very difficult time during and after my divorce. I felt like a failure because I couldn't make my marriage work. I understood very deeply how different my life was from the lives of my neighbors and co-workers. That difference created a barrier. How wonderful it would have been if a teacher or neighbor had put their arm around my children and asked if they needed anything. Just something simple like a smile or a kind word can make a child and adult's day so much better. It shows you are not judging them but instead care about them. All I could try to do was to make sure they knew how much I loved them and help them whenever they needed it.

CHAPTER FIVE

The Downward Spiral Continues

S OME OF THE FINANCIAL STRESS EASED. THE DIVORCE AND VIOLENCE were put further and further behind me. David's move out of state had put an end to the regular physical and emotional abuse and conflict. My emotions were not so raw. As I improved so did the children. Our life started to have some measure of peace and joy. It was definitely improving, albeit with a few traumas still.

"Mom, I don't want to go to visit Dad!" Jessica screamed.

"You have to. We don't have a choice. It is court-ordered visitation," I replied. As she and Ellen were walking up the ramp to board the plane Jessica threw up all over the ramp.

"I don't want to go," she shrieked. She ran back down the ramp and clung to me. I watched as the flight attendant escorted my little five-year old daughter onto the plane. Ellen was so excited. Their father rarely asked to see any of them. I knew that if I denied him the rare visits he requested, he would resume where he had left off with the threats of kidnapping and violence. I let Ellen go. Jessica stayed home with me. Samuel wasn't asked to visit his father. Ellen had a wonderful visit, but then, she always was her father's favorite.

In addition to David there were persons that could upset the balance I was finally finding. Unfortunately, I had a difficult time when my parents would come to visit once or twice a year as they had done before my divorce. I loved that they came to see their grandkids, but it was difficult dealing with my mother. She would cook dinner every night, and when I arrived home from work it would be on the table. We would all sit down to eat dinner together which is a ritual I have always loved. That part was absolutely wonderful. Unfortunately, my mother would also make a huge mess of the kitchen and leave it for me to clean up. It wasn't just a few dirty dishes. The sink would be piled high with dirty pots and pans. The counters were covered with food debris. She would even drop food on the floor and leave it there. She loved to bake with the kids and when making things like peanut brittle she would drop sticky things on the floor and leave them there. She would allow things in the pans to splatter on the stove and not clean them up so they would cook and become hard on the top of the stove. I tried to talk to her about it like having the kids help her clean up the kitchen. But she would get up and simply walk away. I would spend the next hour or two after we finished eating dinner cleaning the kitchen. This was a scene that was repeated every night they were visiting. Their visits were usually about two weeks. I would tell myself it didn't matter because they were spending time with and helping the kids so much, but it wasn't helping me.

My parents never asked me about my life—work, the divorce, or how I was doing. To this day they have never asked anything about that time or really any other time in my life. They were there for the children and I was thankful for the help.

"You spend too much time at the office. Spending time at home with your children is more important than making money or spending a lot of time at the office," my dad would say to me.

"You know only idiots watch TV," he would say at night as I finally sat down for some stress-free time. My dad was generally such a kind and compassionate person but, for a time in his life and as many of us do, he treated others a bit better than his own family. I can't explain exactly how, but they would give me the message that I was a bad mother. They never said it directly, but that has never been their style. They prefer subliminal messages that they can deny if you try to address the issue with them. They would exchange that knowing look that my children were having difficulties and it was because I was a bad mother. They were there to rescue my children from me. If I were able to trust my instincts, I would have been able to recognize the subliminal messages my children and I were receiving from my parents. There was always a shroud of dishonesty around my parents and their interactions with me.

They would undermine my discipline with the children. When I would discipline the children, my father would simply ignore the consequence I had meted out. He wouldn't discuss the situation with me. He just did what he wanted to do with the children. They were more out of control when he was around, especially Samuel.

During one of their bi-yearly visits, I had to question my mother's motives. "What are you knitting, Mom?" I asked her one Saturday morning. She had been ferociously working on this project since she arrived for her visit.

"I am knitting a sweater for David," she replied. "He loves the color blue, and I think he will able to use it on those cold mornings when he goes to play golf. I can't wait to give it to him for Christmas." She went on a for a few more minutes extolling the sweater and David. "Do you think he will like it?" she asked me. I was flabbergasted. David and I had been divorced for more than a few years. I simply walked away. I have no idea if she ever gave it to him.

I would get "sick" every time my parents visited and spend a lot of time in my bedroom lying in bed. I figured that I was very tired and it was good to rest now that I had some help. Maybe that was part of it, but I later came to realize that it was a way of avoiding interaction with my parents.

"Why have you been so upset these last few days?" my assistant, Melissa, asked me. I guess I was more nervous than usual.

"My mother is coming to visit. She really stresses me out," I replied.

"Just tell her not to come," Melissa replied. "You don't have to put yourself through that," she said. It sounded so simple when she said it. Could I do that? I wondered. I really didn't want to hurt my parents' feelings. This was my first real lesson in self-compassion. Melissa was a pretty unlikely teacher of self-compassion, but I have learned lessons can come from all different places if we are open to them. She herself was a bit of an emotional disaster.

I agonized over what to do for several days. My anxiety increased dramatically as the day of my mother's visit approached. Finally, I called my mother. It took a week or so for me to get up my nerve.

As soon as she answered the phone, I said, "Don't come to visit me." I immediately hung up the phone. I didn't give her an opportunity to say anything. It was a terribly cruel thing to do. Neither she nor my father ever called me back then or at any other time for more than two years. I didn't do it because I understood I needed to practice self-compassion. That was such a foreign concept for me and one I wouldn't really understand for many years to come. My litmus test at the time was that if an event or person rendered me incapable of functioning then I should eliminate or avoid that person or event. I guess that was a crude form of self-compassion. I wasn't going to be able to function with my mother's criticism and judgmental attitude. I really hadn't learned how to kindly and firmly communicate my limits to anyone, much less my parents, so they are not totally responsible for treating me badly. I had a responsibility to myself to communicate with them which I failed to do. To be honest, I don't think they would have listened, but I still should have tried.

My mother has always treated my children much better than she ever treated my sister or me. When they were little, she was very kind, patient, and loving. In part, I had maintained a close connection with my parents because I thought it was good for my children. I didn't want to deprive my children of the love of their grandparents, but I felt I had no choice but to cancel her visit. I really expected the respite to be very brief. I expected that at some point in time, my parents would call, and we would talk about why I did what I did. They never called. I could have called, but I didn't have the strength to battle judgment, criticism, and their wall of silence.

This break from my parents helped me to recognize some of the detrimental behaviors they engaged in as parents. The inability to communicate with them about anything was the most frustrating. Their way of ignoring what I said, how I felt, or what I wanted, even as an adult, was what ultimately caused the break. Often my parents thought they were helping me out, when in fact they were not. Once

I saw more clearly, I was able to work to stop acting that same way in parenting my own children.

This break from my parents would help me to heal more of the heartache of my childhood. I needed a break from the constant criticism and judgment of my parents. I was still dealing with the fallout of my divorce. Their behavior was like pouring salt into an open wound. I felt free to learn a different way of parenting. I would also need to learn to stop judging my parents for their shortcomings as I hoped my children would not judge me for mine.

I worried about the effect of this estrangement from my parents on my children. I felt awful depriving them of the love of their grandparents. "It isn't healthy to allow your parents to treat you disrespectfully in front of your children. It eventually may result in your children feeling like it is okay to treat you that way as well," Dr. M., the psychologist, told me. I had some support and comfort in taking a break from my relationship with my parents. Since my parents lived all the way across the country, I don't think it had as much of an impact on my children as I feared at the time.

As the years passed without any contact with my parents, I was convinced that what I wanted or how I felt was not important to my parents. As I have matured I have come to realize that they just couldn't deal with any emotional issues. Perhaps, knowing and accepting the truth of that is a part of compassion.

We didn't speak to each other for more than two years. I finally initiated the contact. Brian, my future husband, urged me to do it. It was the right thing to do. My parents and I have never spoken about that time. We have never even acknowledged that we didn't speak to each other for several years. Maybe it is too painful for them. When they came back into our lives, they treated me with much more respect. That is what I wanted for me and for the sake of my children.

I realize now that it was good for the children to see me set limits on my parents. Children are aware of so much more than we think they are. In setting limits on my parents, I was learning self-compassion although I had no idea that was what I was doing. I was just trying to survive still. I was beginning to care for myself and to attend to my own needs rather than always putting the needs of others ahead of my own. I am still learning how to be compassionate with myself. Later, I would develop a genuine compassion for my parents but that would take many more years. Then our relationship would be healed.

CHAPTER SIX

A Second Chance at Love

I STARTED ATTENDING LAW SCHOOL WHEN JESSICA WAS FOURTEEN months old. Samuel was born in the middle of my fourth semester, and I was pregnant with Ellen last semester. Ellen was born shortly after I took the bar exam. By the time I obtained my divorce from David. I had been working as an attorney for about three or four years.

"Are you married? Do you have any children? How many? What are their ages? Who takes care of the children while you are at work? What do you do when your child is sick? What does your husband do for a living?" the interviewer shot the questions off in a rapid-fire manner reminding me of a firing squad. I answered each one honestly and just as rapidly giving no explanation. He wasn't the first or last interviewer to ask me those questions. I remember thinking how hard I had worked to obtain all this education and how everything boiled down to whether I had children and what my husband did for a living.

"You were naïve to answer those questions. It is illegal to ask them," my friend, to whom I was relating this story many years later, said indignantly and angrily. Was I naïve, or was I a realist regarding the job market of those times? I knew I couldn't hide the fact that I had three young children for very long. What was the alternative? This was 1982 in the rust belt and the time of the first exodus of women law school graduates into the job market. I responded simply to my friend, "You haven't looked for work in really dire economic times, have you?"

I never dreamed of being a lawyer. I had a few dreams of accomplishment when I was in high school, but I allowed those to be smashed and never replaced them. I fell into going to law school. I saw it as a good way to make a living to help support my family. At that time, I really wanted to stay home and be with my children. In many ways I am glad I didn't get what I wished for. I am grateful to David for supporting me while I attended law school.

One of my fellow summer law clerks had a prescient observation. "What does your husband do for a living?" he asked. My husband did not have a glamorous or well-paying job. I answered the question. "He is supporting you through law school so he can retire when you graduate," was the response from him. At the time I thought that was a pretty cynical view of marriage. Sadly, it turned out that he was very intuitive. David virtually stopped working shortly after I found my first job as a lawyer. He didn't want to be a house husband either. He wanted to devote himself to playing golf.

"Can you type? Do you know shorthand? Do you know your alphabet well enough to be able to file documents accurately? Are you willing to take a typing and general skills test?" asked the representative at the temporary employment agency. I was about seven months pregnant and they were the only place that wouldn't care about that.

"Could you send me to a law firm if possible?" I asked. I didn't tell her why. I didn't want her to know that I had just graduated from law school and couldn't find a job. The employment agency placed me in a job. I answered phones. I typed. I filed documents. I kept track of the attorneys' calendars. After a few months I left to have my third child. "Call me after you have the baby, and we will see if we have some work for you as a lawyer," the senior partner told me.

A few weeks after the baby was born, I called him. He hired me. At my first job as a lawyer I was nothing more than a glorified clerk making eight dollars an hour three days a week. I was grateful. Silly because I don't think the pay even covered my child care expenses, but I thought it would lead to something better. We were broke, but I had to start somewhere.

My introduction on the first day was a precursor to how I would be treated at the firm. "I told you she was pretty. Pregnancy makes you swell and retain water," the senior partner said to the junior partner as I sat in his office. This was my first day on the job as a lawyer, and I was being welcomed to the law firm.

I wasn't treated with very much respect by anyone but especially by the legal secretaries. Laurie, the senior secretary, refused to talk to me and refused to do any work for me. I would ask her a question and she would turn her back on me and walk out of the room. This happened several times in the presence of the senior partner. He recognized it but said I should just accept it. (Some twenty years later, I was told the same thing by another senior partner.) I just had to put up with it. I needed a job to support my family and I needed some experience if I was going to get a better job. I naively believed that hard work and being good at what I did would bring financial rewards and job stability. I worked at this firm for about a year when the senior partner decided he wanted to hire a man who was of the same religious faith as the senior partner. I was fortunate to find a better job, so it worked out for the best.

At the new job I wasn't paid as well as the male attorney who I found out left because he didn't do much work. He would come into the office and read the newspaper and talk on the phone. I know this because I became friends with the support staff. I was watched like a hawk.

There was no future in law or probably much else in the rust belt, so I left my hometown and moved out west to where there were plenty of jobs and cheap housing. I went through an interview where the two male partners asked me the same questions regarding my family. I took the job with them because it was the first one that was offered to me. It was pretty scary moving three small children to a new city all the way across the country when I had no job, but it worked out. David and I were still married at the time although we divorced shortly after our move.

"I have seen many attorneys spend a lot more hours at the office than you but I have never seen anyone work as hard as you when they are here," the senior partner said to me. This was a very small law firm. I worked like a maniac from the minute I walked in the door until I left. I churned out the work and the billable hours. I rarely ate lunch and rarely socialized. I didn't think I had any choice. If I wanted to keep my job, that is. I had to compensate somehow for the fact that I couldn't stay longer hours if I wanted to spend any time with my children.

I usually left the office about six in the evening. The other three male lawyers were still there when I left. They would throw me disappointed looks and sometimes even ask why I wasn't staying later. I did stay late a few times to see what I was missing out on. I wanted to be sure I was somehow compensating during the day for the extra hours I didn't put in at night. I discovered that as soon as the support staff left, the lawyers started to socialize. There wasn't any work being done. Every now and then one of the lawyers would say he had to run to his office to finish something he had failed to finish earlier that day. In reality I'm not sure they wanted me there, but they wanted me to think they did. That way when it came time to negotiate raises they could hold that against me. They never said it, but they didn't have to. I was angry because I knew my failure to stay late had nothing to do with the quantity or the quality of the work I did. Yet it was still held against me. As a woman with three young children, I was expected to show an attitude of appreciation for having been given a job. I showed my appreciation by working harder than my male counterparts. I had to prove myself in more ways than males who had three children.

At a small law firm, you get more responsibility as there is a lot of work and only a few lawyers to cover it. I was able to get to court early on in my career and to get a good bit of trial experience. The partners at this small firm did not discriminate against me in that regard. I am grateful for that.

"Come into the judge's chambers. He will conduct the pre-trial conference in there," the bailiff informed the attorneys where we were waiting in the courtroom. Opposing counsel and I entered the judge's chambers. The judge was seated at his desk. We sat down in the chairs facing the judge.

The judge was looking at what appeared to be the case file when we entered. Without looking up he said, "This is the time set for the pre-trial conference." He looked up from his desk. His whole demeanor changed when he saw me. Looking directly at me, he said angrily, "Trial counsel was ordered to appear at this conference."

"I am trial counsel, your honor," I replied somewhat shakily.

"You can't be," was the icy response. I sheepishly sat down. The judge was definitely not pleased. The trial was set to begin in a few weeks. It was a rough experience.

I was working at this small firm when things began to fall apart with David. I tried to hide it. People at the office knew something was wrong, but I continued to put out the work so no questions were asked. I wondered if I should say something about the divorce or not. I really needed this job especially now. I could not afford to be fired. Would I be able to hide the situation from them? If I could hide it would I be better off? After weeks of agony, and I didn't need any more of that, I finally decided I needed to tell them. I was raised with "honesty is always the best policy" although I have come at times to doubt the wisdom of that teaching.

"If we thought you might be getting a divorce we never would have hired you. Employees going through a divorce are always less productive and bring a lot of angst into the office," said one partner.

The other partner continued, "Who is going to help with your kids now? How are you going to work here as a single mother of three children?" He was very angry.

"Well, at least I didn't get fired," I thought. I knew there was absolutely no way I could let my personal issues or any issues with my children interfere with my work. I wouldn't be able to take any time off. I couldn't take any of my one week of vacation time for a while. They watched me like a hawk for a while after that to make sure that my personal and child rearing issues did not interfere with my productivity. The pressure at the office was, at times, overwhelming. I was in no position to complain. Needless to say, law firms, especially at that time, were not bastions of compassion. Everything was measured by how productive you were. As one of the partners used to say, "You are only as good and as valuable as the last trial you won." I am happy to see that attitudes are changing. Recently some employers have begun discussing ways to incorporate compassion into the workplace because it is good for the bottom line. It certainly wasn't even remotely a topic back then.

"Do you have a place I can leave Jessica next week? She has to have oral surgery to have twelve teeth removed. I can't miss any work to stay home with her," I said to the administrator at the summer day camp she was attending.

"We can set up a cot for her in the room adjacent to my office," she replied.

On the appointed day, I dropped Jessica off at the summer camp with her mouth swollen, bleeding, and stuffed with gauze. I laid her on the cot. Jessica didn't complain about staying at the summer camp. She was always such a trooper. As I laid her down, she was still sleepy from the medication. "Hopefully the pain medication they gave her will allow her to sleep all day until I pick her up," I said to myself. As I drove to the office, I felt overwhelmed by worry about Jessica and guilt over what a terrible mother I was. I believed I was the worst mother in the world that day or, should I say, especially on that day. I think I always felt like that back then. It is just that some days the guilt was worse than others. This was definitely one of those days.

As a working mother, especially a single working mother, I felt an overwhelming burden of guilt and hopelessness. Guilt was my constant companion. I wasn't a good enough mother or lawyer. And when I was married I wasn't a good enough wife. I was never good enough at anything. I could never raise successful children. My life was a constant juggling act. How could I possibly compete with the mothers of my children's friend who were stay at home moms? I resented stay-at-home mothers. They had some free time of themselves, time to really spend with their children, and a partner who among other things provided financial support. I was angry because their lives were so much easier than mine.

Sadly, we women had so much to offer each other, but we didn't. We focused on what divided us rather than what united us. We were entrenched in our enemy camps. We were after all mortal enemies. At the heart of the battle was the working moms' resentment and the conviction by stay-at-home moms that only full time mothers could raise successful, well-adjusted children and have successful marriages. I think they feared that all they had sacrificed would be in vain if working moms could do the same. Their choices and existence were only justified if they produced better results than the working mothers. The principal measure of their success were their children and the financial success of their husbands. Success in children was measured by academic and athletic achievement and conforming behavior. If working mothers could do it too what was left for them? How could they justify their choice and all they had sacrificed?

If only we had been able to muster a little compassion for each other. If we could have put ourselves in the shoes of the other and seen first-hand their struggles and issues. If we could have talked about and shared our lives. I thought their lives were easier. They thought my life was glamorous as I got to get dressed up and went somewhere important every day. As I have matured, I realized their life, in many ways, really wasn't easier, but I didn't understand that back then when my children were very young. Their choices came with price tags just as mine did. How I wish I could have been aware of that back then. We might have been able to find some common ground and some connection. We could have supported each other and shown each other compassion instead of judging and criticizing each other.

At work, it took a lot of energy to navigate the competing demands of clients, bosses, judges, and opposing counsel. I learned early on that being too assertive or demanding would just make the judge or opposing counsel angry and backfire. At some level I had to engage in some socially acceptable female conduct. The expectation was different with each judge or opposing counsel. How I wished I could just show up and be a guy—an assertive advocate for my client. Oh, sure they had to tailor their argument to the particular judge, but at least they didn't have to tailor their personality in order to be heard. Most judges expected some level of subservience or attitude of deference—kind of being grateful to them for allowing you, a woman, to be in his courtroom.

I had always been pretty much a pushover. I went along with what other people wanted. Being a single mother and a litigation attorney changed all of that. I learned to stand up for myself and my children. I developed my tough side. I was always tough in getting through difficult times, but I had never been tough in defending or expressing myself. All of that changed now. It was a process to find the balance. I am grateful to my mother because she helped me develop that toughness as a child, and it saved my life as an adult. Being compassionate does not mean you are a doormat. Of course learning to stand up for yourself in the workplace is not the same as setting limits for yourself in the community and in your family. It took a much longer time for me to practice self-compassion with my children and spouse. Being tough is a part of being compassionate too, but that is a lesson I really didn't learn until I and to deal with my troubled teens.

This was the backdrop of my life when I met Brian. We met through work. We didn't work at the same company. Our paths just randomly crossed, and we were thrown together working toward what eventually became a common goal. Brian is the one who transformed an adversarial situation into a cooperative business venture from which we could both benefit. He had a real knack for and intuition for bringing people together in a business setting.

From my observations it seems that it is exactly those qualities that make people successful in the business world that make them unsuccessful in their personal life. Brian was, to put it mildly, a very intense and demanding person. He was also very charismatic and charming. I was a little put off by his intensity. If he wanted something, it was no holds barred, and for some reason, he wanted to have a relationship with me. It was a little scary but also very flattering. I wasn't playing hard to get. After my experiences with David, I wasn't the least bit interested in having another relationship.

During the four or five years Brian and I dated, we were able to evaluate, somewhat rationally, all the baggage that came along with the other person. He could readily see that I had three very young children. He had one young child. It was not so easy to identify our respective emotional and relationship issues. Still, during that time we were able to see each other with all our warts. There was something between us that made us want to connect in spite of our issues. That desire made us willing to work on connecting with each other. Why we were both so willing to do such hard work is still a mystery to me. There was something that brought us and held us together. At the time I wondered if that something was a genuine and enduring love for each other.

In the beginning, we didn't let the children know we were seeing each other. We started our relationship as friends going out to lunch together or meet briefly after work if I had a sitter. Brian would call me at the office or late at night at home after the children were in bed. We saw each other mostly at lunchtime.

I'm glad I had learned to keep my relationship with Brian a secret from the children for a while. I didn't want them to experience any of the ups and downs a relationship can have. I had made a mistake briefly before and I did not want to repeat it. As our relationship intensified, it played out in fits and starts. Brian and I would fight, break up, and then get back together. It was typical behavior for two people how had prior failed marriages, but I realize now how incredibly immature we were acting toward each other.

Finally, we had settled into a strong commitment, and it was time for us to meet each other's children. Brian invited all of us to spend the day at the local waterpark. He brought his daughter, Bridget, and I brought my three. It was an easy, fun day. My children stuck close to me and avoided interacting much with Brian and his daughter. Still I thought the first meeting between Brian and my children was successful. Brian didn't try to force interaction with the children. I did the same with his daughter. We both had prior experience in relating to stepchildren, and it wasn't a positive experience. I remember thinking that day that maybe we were on the right track. The children and I didn't talk about Brian or his daughter on the ride home. I didn't bring it up since they didn't seem to want to discuss it. I wanted them to accept him and yes, if things worked out with Brian, I hoped one day they might even love him. I knew I could not force the acceptance and certainly not the love. It would have to develop slowly.

I thought I could face any situation alone. At least I had convinced myself that I could. I had to because I really had no other options. It was just the reality of my life back then. I had no safety net—no support emotionally or financially in the days when my children were very young.

So I was surprised that my invincibility was shaken by this upcoming event. I was afraid it might turn into a confrontation. Brian was taking all of us—the children and I—to meet his family for the first time. He was very close to his family. We were going to spend Thanksgiving at his sister Nancy's house. She had five children. Brian was bringing his daughter, Bridget, and I was bringing my three.

By this time, we had already met many of Brian's friends and taken the kids with us to business events that included family and friends. People fussed over Bridget. She was the center of attention. I remember one of my first experiences occurred when we were all invited to dinner by one of Brian's clients. We were going to this great Western steakhouse. This was the kind of place I couldn't afford to take my children in those days. It was going to be a real treat for them. They were excited and so was I. Brian and Bridget came to pick us up. When we arrived at the restaurant, our hosts Bob and Kim were already there. They were waiting at the entrance for us. Kim came running over as we approached. She grabbed Bridget and hugged her. She started asking her all about school, her mom, etc. I was waiting for the greeting to finish so I could introduce myself and my children to her. The greeting never finished. Brian and Bob talked business at one end of the table. Bridget sat next to Kim. My children and I sat at the far end of the table. Bridget and Kim chatted and laughed together throughout the evening. Kim ordered special drinks and desserts for Bridget. Brian seemed oblivious to all of this.

At the beginning of the evening I tried to converse with Kim, but it was like penetrating a thick wall. I tried to engage my children in some conversation, but they were all silent during dinner. I sat wondering if there was any way to confront Kim or anyone else about this treatment without looking petty or jealous. If there was a way, I never discovered it. After all, maybe I was just being petty and jealous? I know that I expect too much of people. I expected Kim to be a gracious hostess. She wasn't, and I didn't know how to deal with that. As I look back, I should just have asserted myself there as I had to do in the business world, but I didn't know how to do that yet in a social situation.

So I prepared myself for a similar experience at Brian's sister's house. I knew that she was a close friend of Bridget's mother. I didn't want to get all defensive, but I didn't want my children to continually receive that same message of inferiority. I spent the drive going over several scenarios in my mind as to how I would protect my children—even if it meant being confrontational.

At that time, I naively thought this disparity in treatment would pass as time went on. But in the years to come, Brian and I would have many a heated argument over this issue. There was definitely a subliminal message that my children were second class citizens compared to Bridget. She was prettier, smarter, better behaved than my kids or so the message went. Brian said it wasn't happening and that I was overly sensitive. I went along with that for a while in part because I doubted myself and my perceptions. Other people in our business and social world simply didn't care, were blind to it or ignored it and went along with Brian's program. Unfortunately, my children weren't blind to it.

It really hurt to see my children treated like this especially when they would look at me with eyes that said I was supposed to protect them. It took me a while to trust myself. I am not exactly sure when I finally did get it. I had a huge sense of guilt for letting it go on for so long.

I braced myself for the worst. Brian entered his sister's house first. I heard someone greet him. As soon as I walked through the door I was smothered with a big hug. "Welcome, welcome. We are so glad you could be here for Thanksgiving!"

I looked up to see Brian's sister, Nancy, beaming a huge smile at me. Each of my children received a similar welcome. Nancy started talking to me as if she had known me for years. She introduced my children to her brood and invited them to make themselves right at home, which they did. It was a wonderful holiday. I noticed that Bridget hung back a little. I guess that she wasn't used to not being the center of attention. I felt bad for her. My children were having a great time hanging out with the cousins.

While we were in the middle of our Thanksgiving meal, there was a knock at the door. Nancy jumped up from her chair and ran over to greet a woman. The woman was dressed in tight pants and a top that didn't cover her navel. She had platinum blond hair, purple fingernail polish, bright blue eye shadow, and black lipstick. She was accompanied by a small skinny toddler dressed in clothes that were a few sizes too small for him. Nancy turned and announced their arrival. "This is Kevin, my grandson and Deanna, his mother. This is Eric's son." I knew something of the family history from Brian. Eric wasn't married and never had been. He had a drinking problem and couldn't hold a job, or so I had been told.

"Deanna is an alcoholic and drug addict. She claims Kevin is Eric's son, but I am not sure. She and Eric were together only very briefly. Deanna has trouble holding a job. She and Kevin were homeless for a while, and they stayed here. She is doing better now, but she hangs out with other drug addicts, and I worry about Kevin," Nancy said. She spoke as if she was reciting ingredients in a recipe. I kept waiting to hear it—the judgment, the contempt for Deanna, her lifestyle and her inability to be a competent mother to Kevin. But all I detected in Nancy's demeanor and tone of voice was love and concern for Deanna and Kevin.

I was shocked that Nancy would fuss over Kevin like she did her other grandchildren! I remember thinking at the time that people like Deanna, who engage in this type of behavior, need to have some consequence so others will be deterred from such conduct. At a minimum, shouldn't Deanna, and by implication, Kevin, be ostracized or at least treated with a little disdain as some consequence? That is what I was brought up to believe and the attitude that would unconsciously surface. What a mean spirited hypocrite I was! Wasn't I just ecstatic that Nancy didn't treat my children any differently because I was divorced?

"She was all about love. She didn't have a mean bone in her body," Samuel said between sobs. He has always been very sensitive. This was many, many years after we first met Nancy. We were standing together at the cemetery for Nancy's funeral service. "How true," I thought. My eldest son was just a child when he spent a lot of time with Nancy, yet her message of love and compassion reached him. He learned to practice it too in his adult life.

Nancy welcomed everyone into her home and her heart. She had health problems that were beyond horrible. She had serious issues with her own children. Yet she always smiled. She never rarely complained. She was ever so grateful for what she did have. Most of us wrote her off as a nut case because she was constantly talking about death and illness in great detail. "She was out of touch with the real world," we said to ourselves. I guess she was out of touch with the way the world worked. She wasn't judgmental. She didn't treat people differently based on their lifestyle, mistakes, or history. Nancy lived her Christian faith. She was all about compassion—showing love without judgment, accepting and caring about everyone whatever their circumstance in life was, and forgiving people for their mistakes rather than punishing them. We watched as they lowered her casket into the ground. She had always been there for me. I would sorely miss her. Her love and compassion enveloped you and could take the cares of the world away.

With Brian it was wonderful to finally have some adult companionship and support. It was a relief to have someone to share the responsibilities and stresses of life. I think the fact that we saw and acknowledged each other's warts made us love each other more. We didn't have to be expending all our energy trying to be, pretending to be perfect, or protecting our perfect image. We were slowly tearing away our respective protective shrouds to reveal our true selves to each other. Romance, infatuation, and all the baggage we bring to relationship can be transformed into real love. It is of course a process. Brian and I were working on that.

The children were excited that Brian and I were going to get married, although I'm sure they had their concerns. Brian seemed to love my children from the very first day he met them at the waterpark. From the very beginning he treated them as if they were his own. I was so appreciative of his love for them and I loved him for that. Maybe when you really love the other person, you love what they love or all that comes with them. That is not to say we didn't have issues between us regarding the children, just that they didn't derail our relationship permanently as they had the potential to do. I think I wanted to marry Brian because of the way he treated my children and because he was a good provider. I thought he would be a good father and husband. He must have really good values if he was willing to take on three young children. Life had a lot to teach me about my feelings for Brian and love. In the end I was very surprised.

Brian and I set our wedding date out about six months. That would give me time to sell my house. Brian's house was newer and bigger, so we were going to move in with him. Life became absolutely crazy as the wedding day approached. A big litigation case I had been handling got set for a six-week trial to begin about eight weeks before the wedding. I sold my house earlier than expected, and the buyer would not let us rent it from him for a month. So the children and I had to move in with Brian before the wedding—something I did not want to do.

During the time before the wedding, Brian's dad's health deteriorated, and he was in the hospital. The entire last year had been a roller coaster of ups and downs regarding his father's health. Brian was very close to his father. The bedside vigil at the hospital went on for weeks. Brian and I were at the hospital every evening during that time. Brian went during the day also. Several times I had been called saying, if possible, I needed to come right away as the end was imminent. I would call the children from the hospital to check on whether homework was done and preparations ready for school the next day. I kissed them all good night over the phone. Then I went back to the bedside vigil. We were all there—Brian, me, his sister Nancy, and her husband Bob. After a couple of weeks of this, his father's condition worsened.

"You don't need to do that," Nancy said to the young hospital respiratory technician. She had just placed an oxygen mask over their father's mouth to start some treatment. "He's dying," Nancy continued. The poor young girl looked like a fawn that had just looked into the headlights of an oncoming car. She took her machine and slithered out of the room.

"How could Nancy know that their father was dying?" I asked myself. A few minutes later Brian put his face down on the bed next to his father's lifeless body. I couldn't move. I didn't know how to comfort Brian. After a short time, Brian pulled himself together, and he and Nancy left the room where they made the arrangements for the body. For me it was something of a relief. Our wedding was to take place in less than a month, but for now we had to plan a funeral. As you can imagine the strain of all these huge life events took a toll on our relationship.

I remember it so clearly. Brian and I were sitting on the couch in the TV room of the first house we lived in together. The children were in their bedrooms getting ready for bed. I have no recollection of what was said. Brian and I exchanged angry words. I decided I couldn't marry him.

I decided to leave. I had no idea at that time what drove me to do that. I am sure I convinced myself it was something Brian said or did. As I look back on it, I think I was driven by fear. I wanted the security and comfort of marriage, but I was afraid of many things including what marrying Brian would mean to my independence and identity. Brian had very traditional ideas about marriage. What price would I have to pay to be married? A huge conflict was raging in me.

"Get your stuff together right now. We are leaving!" I shouted as I opened each of the doors to my children's respective bedrooms. They didn't question me. While they gathered up their stuff, I gathered up some of my clothing. We threw our stuff into the minivan, and we drove to a hotel where we would spend the first of several nights. I drove the children to school the next morning, and then I went to court for the trial I was handling. In a few days we would move into a rental house. As I pulled away from Brian's house that night I looked in the rear view mirror. I saw Brian standing at the front door. He was still very angry but also incredulous. I was so selfish I didn't even think about the price my children would pay for my erratic behavior. Oh, my poor children! They have so much to forgive me for!

Brian initiated contact after we left. He called me at the office and asked if we could meet. He came over to the rental house one evening after the children were in bed. We sat outside and talked. I don't remember all the details of that conversation. We did decide to go through with the wedding as planned. We were married a few weeks later, and afterwards we moved back into Brian's house.

Samuel was elated to have a dad but not elated enough to accept discipline very well. Ellen was young enough that she was happy she had a dad. She accepted direction from Brian better than Samuel did, at least for a time. Jessica coped by having many friends that were the center of her world and with whom she spent almost all her time. She made sure she didn't do anything that would require Brian to discipline her. And Brian faithfully stuck to his visitation schedule with Bridget. She spent every other weekend, one evening during the week, certain holidays, and sometime in the summer with us.

Life in the early years of our marriage was so incredibly busy. Brian had a business to run. I was still working full time as a litigation attorney.

"Time to get up," I heard Brian say as he gently shook me.

"I must have slept through the alarm," I thought as I opened my eyes. I went downstairs.

"Jessica, are you up?" I said through her closed bedroom door. She was always up, but I wanted to be sure. I went across the hall. "Ellen, time to get up." Then I knocked on Samuel's door. "Samuel, time to get up." After I made my rounds I went back to my bedroom to get dressed for the office. I had to go back a few times to be sure Ellen and Samuel were actually up and getting ready for school. They had a tendency to fall back to sleep. This morning was no exception. "Get up, get dressed, and get some breakfast now," I said firmly. "I don't want you to miss the school bus."

"Goodbye, Mom," I heard Jessica say.

"Bye," I said.

"Goodbye. Call me later," Brian said as he gave me a kiss goodbye. I had to give some more nudging to Samuel and Ellen. I finally got them out the door to the school bus.

I went back to finish getting ready for work. I heard the door open a few minutes later. "We missed the bus," Ellen said. Ugh. That meant I would be late for work.

"Get in the car, and let's go," I said rather angrily. There was no time to clean up the kitchen. I dropped the kids off at school and raced down the freeway to work.

Alicia greeted me at the office. "Don't forget we have to finish the Carter matter this morning, and you have a meeting at two o'clock this afternoon but not at this office." I picked up my phone messages and glanced through them as I walked to my office.

"Can you come in here for a minute?" I heard my boss say to me.

About forty-five minutes later, I left the senior partner's office to face the pile of files on my desk. The phone rang. It was a client.

Later that morning, I was able to give Brian a quick call. "Hey, don't forget we have a dinner meeting tonight with the representatives of that company whose work I am trying to get," Brian reminded me. Oh Lord!

I was going over in my head how I would get home, get the kids settled in to do homework, get them something to eat, be back downtown in time for dinner with Brian at seven-thirty, and then home in time to review homework and get them to bed on time. When the evening was over, I fell into bed about eleven o'clock. I forgot to say good night to Brian. As soon as my head hit the pillow I was asleep. That used to drive Brian crazy because he wanted some time together with me at night. It just wasn't possible very often.

Brian's business was the center of his world when we met. He was out almost every night of the week attending some business event, sporting event, etc. When we married he expected me to accompany him to all of those events. That meant since I was working full time I would rarely be home with the children. I tried to talk to Brian about this and discuss picking and choosing only certain events I would attend. He simply ignored my requests. Finally, I rebelled. It took some time because Brian did not take no easily. Any no on my part meant there would be a huge fight. I didn't always have the energy for that so I had to pick and choose my fights carefully. As I look back I realize I have sought out, unconsciously, relationships that generate a great deal of adversity and conflict. My marriage to Brian was no exception. It could be characterized as the battle of the wills. We were both very strong-willed people.

"I am not one of your employees," I used to say to Brian. "You can't order me around and tell me what to do all the time." Brian was a very successful businessman. He was forceful. He would push to get things done. I admired those qualities most of the time. Sometimes he would push too hard. Sometimes he just didn't know when I really knew what I wanted or what I didn't want. I didn't blame him for all of that because most of the time I didn't know what I wanted either. If I did know, I was afraid to express my expectations for fear they would not be honored. Or I just felt guilty or selfish for expressing what I wanted. I didn't want to appear too demanding or unfeminine. That attitude wreaked a lot of havoc for me at home and in the business world. It was difficult for me to navigate those waters. I can't imagine how difficult it must have been for Brian.

I felt pulled in so many different directions. I was a mother, a wife, a lawyer, and a stepmother. I was trying to be everything to everyone. Was it any wonder I was often short-tempered, frazzled, and depressed? Since I was raised in a traditional family by a stay-at-home mom, I wanted to raise my children like a stay-at-home mom would. But I didn't have the time or energy to do what the moms of my generation did for their children and their husbands. Still I tried. I wanted to be successful at my career also. I was stretched much too thin to put it mildly. I was not equipped to navigate all these competing demands. I had never known a working mother, so I had no road map to help me navigate the circumstances of my life, including being a stepparent.

We were working to form a family, and by that I mean a group of people who have their differences and issues but who cared enough about each other to work them out. We had a bond, a connection that tied us all together. This may have only been possible because the father of my children had abandoned them. That bond was only disrupted by the regular visits of Bridget.

When Bridget visited, Brian and I would become ensconced in separate camps. How did it become his daughter and him versus my children and me? It definitely didn't start out that way. Somewhere along the way we split apart. As time passed the camps become increasingly separate and hostile.

I can still hear Brian say, "Bridget got straight As." "Bridget got a good-conduct award at school." "Bridget gave up several parties with friends to come for the weekend." "Bridget always does as she is told." At the dinner table the conversation centered on Bridget, her accomplishments, and how wonderful she was. Some things were directly said and some were implied. But the result was the same. Bridget was a better person, student, etc. than my daughters. They were lesser persons than Bridget. I could see it on their faces. I could see it in Brian and Bridget's faces. As I sat at the dinner table, I wondered if I should say something good about my daughters. Didn't that just feed this competition? I didn't want to compete. I didn't want to start a fight. Would anything change if I did say something? The look on the face of my daughters struck like a knife in my heart, especially Ellen. Her self-esteem was so fragile already. I would talk to them later, after dinner. There was a lot of resentment around Bridget—none of which was her doing

"We have to cancel our dinner plans for this coming Saturday with Eloise and Martin," Brian said.

"We have had that planned for weeks," I replied. "Why do we have to cancel?"

"Bridget is coming to visit this weekend, and I don't want to go out while she is here," Brian replied.

"We can go out after she is in bed," I replied. Brian refused to do that. We were always doing things together with the children during the day. But Brian and I could not go out alone at all during the weekends when Bridget visited. I understood that we did not want to go out every weekend, but I resented that our schedule totally revolved around Bridget's visits. This resentment was partly fueled by the fact that when I would try to get out of going to some business event because I wanted to spend some time with my children, Brian would get angry. I thought we could find a little more balance. It seemed totally unfair to me.

"Can you do something special with Bridget this weekend—bake cookies, etc.?" Brian asked. I was expected to make Bridget's visits special. I complied. Some things were said directly by Brian. Most requests were unspoken. Each time she visited, I planned special activities to do with her and for her. We baked cookies and cakes. We sewed. We watched special movies with her. We had outings together. Bridget was the princess and we were all expected to treat her as such. She was a perfect child or so we were told. I don't think Bridget believed this. She didn't for the most part act that way. This was all Brian's doing.

Sadly, a deep connection never developed between Bridget and I. Sometimes I felt she was just putting in her time until she could go home. Bridget's attitude towards me was one of tolerance. I think that was mutual. She was a wonderful child. I often wondered if a bond never developed because Bridget was concerned that if she enjoyed her visits at our house or liked me she would be disloyal to her mother. Maybe I did not want to be disloyal to my children by loving Bridget. Bridget definitely had the power to cause friction between her dad and I, but I don't think that was Bridget's doing. Brian gave her that power. She was after all just a child. For a while, I entertained endless reasons for the friction as I tried to get a handle on the situation and what to do about it. I tried to be compassionate with Bridget as she was in a very difficult situation, but I had to set limits on her behavior. I had to have compassion for my children and what they were going through too. Finding a solution or truce was a long, difficult process.

The children had their struggles with Bridget too. "Bridget told my friends they should hate me," Ellen said through her tears. "Sally wants to go home right now and doesn't want to spend the night because of what Bridget is saying about me," Ellen continued. Ellen was about eight years old at the time. Brian insisted that Ellen and Bridget attend each other's birthday parties. They didn't have any friends in common as we lived in different parts of the city, but they were about the same age. I wasn't sure I believed Ellen at the time, so I talked to two of her friends. They confirmed what Ellen had said. I have to admit I was pretty angry. I also have to admit that there was an element of satisfaction in my anger. I had suspected that Bridget engaged in similar sneaky conduct before, but there was never any proof. I was relieved that my suspicions were confirmed, and I wasn't just being mean. I didn't say anything to Bridget about this.

I went to discuss it with Brian. "I don't believe you. Bridget would never do such a thing," Brian said to me in an angry voice. Brian called Bridget into the room. "Did you try to get Ellen's friends to stop liking her?" he said. Bridget was silent. Brian stormed out of the room. He wasn't really angry at Bridget. He was angry at me because I had refused to sweep this incident under the rug. I never said anything to Brian about this again. He would just get angrier. I checked in with Ellen later, and she said things were going well.

"You are imagining it," Brian said. "You are just jealous that she is a much better kid than any of yours. I don't want to talk about it. You are so petty." All of these things were said at one time or another whenever I tried to talk to Brian about the disparity in treatment between Bridget and my kids. I knew I was not imagining it. Most often he would just storm off in anger when I brought the subject up. It almost destroyed our relationship. It is interesting that this disparity in treatment never happened with Samuel. Maybe that is because Brian didn't have a biological son to compete with or compare to Samuel.

Samuel had his struggles with Brian. He didn't like Brian to discipline him. I appreciated that Brian wanted to and was willing to help raise Samuel and the girls. Ellen was young enough that she loved and respected Brian as her dad. She was hurt when he treated Bridget with kid gloves. Her resentment against Brian may have erupted later, but circumstances made that impossible.

"I want to have a pool party for a group of my eighth grade friends," Jessica said one day. It was summer. It seemed like a good idea. Brian was a little reluctant but agreed to the party. Brian liked to have everything in order, and having a lot of kids over upset the order. The kids arrived, and we let them have the pool and backyard to themselves. We were able to watch, hopefully unnoticed, from the house.

"The kids are standing on the tile edge and diving from the spa into the pool," Brian said rather angrily. I agreed that one of us needed to tell Jessica about this. I thought it could be accomplished simply and quickly. Brian thought otherwise. "Let's go out and talk to Jessica," Brian said.

"Let's not talk to her in front of her friends," I said. I thought it would be best if only one of us went, but Brian insisted on going and I was concerned as to how he would handle it. My concern was justified.

"Jessica, we need to talk to you," Brian said ominously. "Jessica, your friends are too wild. They are destroying the pool and the backyard," Brian said angrily.

Jessica looked at me to see if I agreed. I didn't, and I am sure she saw that in my face. Brian went on angrily for a few moments until I finally convinced him enough had been said. We exchanged some words when we got back to the house. Brian sometimes had the attitude that since it was his house I wouldn't be upset if things were ruined. That wasn't true. I thought we needed to strike a balance between letting the kids have fun and maintaining the house. "Jessica, please don't let your friends stand on the tile and jump from the spa into the pool," would have been enough, I think. Jessica was resentful and angry at me that I gave into Brian. She never had another party at the house.

I felt like I was always walking a tightrope between what Brian considered egregious conduct and the expectations my children had based on my parenting style. Brian was much stricter than I. The children were used to my rules. A lot of things changed when Brian and I married and we all moved in together. This is one area in which Brian didn't want to take things slowly. Brian made me feel like I was giving in too much to my children and being manipulated by them when I didn't agree with his harsher punishments and stricter rules. The children felt like I was Brian's puppet. My children felt like I was betraying them when I sided with Brian. Brian felt like I was betraying him when I sided with my children. I was being tugged in both directions constantly. There was always someone who was mad at me or disappointed with me. Trying to make my marriage work and to blend a family was emotionally exhausting.

"You would never have done that if Brian wasn't around!" Jessica shouted. On many occasions she was right. How could I explain to her that perhaps my parenting skills needed improvement? I had not been the best disciplinarian in part due to the lack of time and energy for it. "Once the children get used to the new rules and lifestyle, things will get easier," I would say to myself. But we needed more than just time to make it all work. I had a premonition that my children would always resent Brian no matter how much time passed. Some of that had to do with Brian, and some just had to do with the nature of the stepparent relationship.

All of this was taking a toll on all of us and on our marriage. Brian and I could not discuss the children or much else about the family without Brian exploding. The anger was always under the surface now, and it was getting worse. Brian became verbally abusive. I felt like I was living with my mother all over again. Nothing the children or I wanted mattered to him. Every time I tried to discuss anything with him about the family, he would explode. It became intolerable, and I finally asked Brian to move out. He refused. The tension and stress were abominable. I took the matter to the courts. Brian was ordered to move out of the house and the children and I had some peace. I wanted to go to marriage counseling. Brian filed for divorce. He served me with the papers at the office. It was embarrassing to say the least. I started shopping around for a new house.

I was still enjoying the peace in my new life when Brian called me at the office. I almost didn't take the call. This was the first time I had seen or spoken to Brian in a few months. He asked me to go to marriage counseling with him. I wasn't sure by then I wanted to go, but I reluctantly agreed. We each went separately to the therapist's office. We sat in separate chairs. The therapist was giving some introductory remarks when Brian blurted out, "I really love you and I want us to stay married." After he said that, Brian bent over in his chair and sobbed uncontrollably. I froze. George, the marriage counselor, waited a moment and then started to talk again. I was thankful that I didn't have to say or do anything. He had moved out of the house and filed for divorce. We had briefly tried marriage counseling before we split up, but it hadn't helped. "Why would this be any different?" I wondered. Then I saw this tough, macho guy sobbing, and I knew this time it would be different.

I think that, for my generation and those that came before, men were expected to keep all of their emotions bottled up, stuffed down. They were permitted to express only one emotion— anger. I think that is why in all of our more intimate conversations, Brian's response was always to get angry. We really couldn't communicate with each other on important issues without one of us getting angry. Brian seemed to only be able to express tenderness and love in our most intimate moments together. Those were moments of unparalleled love and connection.

"When Brian is really angry, I want you to go up and hug him. It is impossible to stay angry at someone when they are touching or hugging you," George, our marriage counselor said.

"There is absolutely no way I can do that. Have you heard me when I told you the incredibly cruel things he says to me when he is angry?" I shot back.

"Yes, I heard you, but when Brian says those terrible things, I want you to look at him and say to yourself that this is my best friend who is in terrible pain. Don't get caught up in what Brian is saying," George replied. I stared at George incredulously.

"There is absolutely no way I can or will do that," I replied.

"Well, you know it takes two to fight," George said to me.

"What the hell does that mean? Do you really think I should just silently by and take all the insults and cruelties without saying anything, without defending myself?" I shrieked.

"Yes," George replied. "Just remember that Brian's anger is usually fueled by something other than what you have done or what you two have discussed. Please try this," George said calmly.

"Why the h*** should I do all of that?" I thought to myself. It is Brian's problem and he should deal with it, not me. Brian was verbally abusive, not me. George should just tell Brian to stop verbally bashing me. I wanted to be able to blame Brian for the struggles in our relationship. I didn't want to take any responsibility for them. I was playing my own blame game. I could be superior and arrogant because my bad behaviors were not so easily recognizable. I didn't get angry and say cruel things but I got the message across in other ways. Brian and I both had much to work on, although my progress would be delayed by my refusal to give up the higher moral ground.

If only we could see others, especially those closest to us, the way George wanted me to see Brian. Why is it so difficult for us to see the anger being expressed by the person we love as an expression of his/her pain? We take it all so personally and react accordingly. I would remember and nurse old hurts and wounds over the mean things Brian had said to me in the past. I wish instead I could have remembered his acts of kindness and love as he vented his anger. I know that would have diffused his anger and the situation. Nursing old hurts and becoming defensive only served to fuel his anger and escalated almost every disagreement to epic proportions. I know this because slowly, I was able to do what George asked. Oh, I can't say I always did it kindly. In the beginning I think it made me feel superior to Brian and more in control. But eventually that faded as well.

This was my first lesson in showing compassion to my spouse. I'm not talking about putting all my needs aside for the other person and living to please that person. That isn't compassion. That is just being a doormat. I am talking about putting myself in the shoes of my spouse. Instead of listening to the cruel and angry words I would envision Brian with a huge amount of pain and hurt inside him that was erupting like a volcano. I wanted to ease that hurt because he was my best friend and we do that for best friends. My compassion was young and raw, but it would eventually grow and mature.

Brian and I were two very dysfunctional people who were trying to form a healthy relationship. We were making progress. You see, in part that is how I knew Brian loved me. He was working hard at making changes in himself for the good of our relationship. I hope he saw the same in me. We were transforming ourselves, each other, and our relationship. Unfortunately, all progress came to a screeching halt due to circumstances beyond our control and all of our old habits resurfaced. Eventually though the compassion I was learning to practice now toward Brian would grow and grow as we faced the challenges ahead. It was compassion that saved our relationship at this time in our lives and it was compassion that would save me and our relationship again later in our marriage.

CHAPTER SEVEN

Finding Compassion for My Parents

Isn't it interesting how what seem like small, routine events end up later having the biggest impact on our lives? This was one of those situations. I made my annual visit to the gynecologist. There was a problem. The doctor asked me to return. It was described to me as potentially very serious, so I asked Brian to come with me.

"You have a condition that will require the removal of your uterus—a hysterectomy. I know that you mentioned to me that you might want to have more children. If you do want another child you should do it now," the doctor said to Brian and me. Brian and I were seated next to each other. We turned, looked at each other, and said yes to each other with our eyes. We seemed to have an ability to communicate without speaking—at least regarding some issues. We never had an actual verbal conversation ever about having a child together. We instinctively knew it was the right thing to do. I had agonized over this decision for several years. In fact, I told Brian when we were dating that I did not want any more children. I knew he did. I said if he wanted more we should stop seeing each other. He never said anything verbally. I would revisit that decision many times over the next several years. I had three healthy children that I had struggled to raise financially, emotionally, and physically. I had been and still was to a certain extent exhausted all the time by the demands of children, work, and marriage. But in that moment I knew it was the right thing to do.

I was thirty-seven years old at that time. Brian was older. Good Lord! That would make five young children between us with the new one being nine-and-a-half years younger than its next closest sibling. Jessica was fourteen, Samuel was twelve, Ellen was almost ten, and Bridget was nine. I figured that by making this decision I added ten years to my full time parenting years.

In the ensuing months of my pregnancy when I would become anxious or question the soundness of my decision, I would remind myself that I would not be doing it all alone this time. I know Brian sensed my fears. He had a knack for reassuring me in a very real way without words. I can't explain it any better than that. Brian was a very involved husband and father. I knew he would share the burdens, responsibilities, and joys with me. I so wanted to share the experience of parenting a child. In addition to shouldering the financial and physical burdens alone, life as a single parent it is a very lonely experience emotionally.

"Everyone, dinner is ready," I called from the kitchen. Everyone arrived at the dinner table and we sat down to eat. My parents were visiting from back East. I had been a nervous wreck all day waiting for this dinner. I didn't eat much as I was anxiously trying to get up my courage. Dinner was almost over. I would have to say something now. Putting it off would only make matters worse. "I'm pregnant!" I announced. All heads spun to look at me. No one said a word. There was an eerie silence. No words of congratulations or excitement were forthcoming, even from my parents. Everyone got up and silently left the table. I didn't take that as a good sign.

My parents were back in our lives. They didn't like Brian much. Oh, they never said anything, but I could tell by the way they treated him that they didn't like him. I have some idea why. My parents used to be able to come out and run the house and the children during my first marriage and my divorce. That stopped when I married Brian. He had strict rules for the children and the running of the house. I did too, but I just didn't have the strength to fight my parents over it. Brian did.

It was around this time as I was really enjoying my family that I started to reflect on the lives of my parents. They talked very little about their respective childhoods but there were a few stories that had surfaced over the years.

"The sheriff posted a foreclosure notice on our front door of our house. It was there when I came home from school one day. You see, my father lost his business. We had already sold our only car and everything else we could sell. We didn't get much because no one had any money to buy anything back then. My mother found a job as a secretary in the next town. She would leave the house at five o'clock a.m. and return about seven thirty p.m. every day. It was an hour- and-a-half train ride from our town to where she worked. In the dark, rain, sleet, and snow she would walk to the train station from our house. Our two ill grand-parents moved into our house. We took care of them. My brother and I slept in the attic because our grandparents occupied our bedrooms. I never heard my mother complain. She knew we were one of the lucky families because we had food, a home, and at least one job. We were rescued from homelessness by a wealthy friend of my father's who paid off the back taxes."

I like to think my mother told me this story about her family, but she didn't. It is a story that I pieced together over many years. Snippets of the events were related by people other than my mother. I think it was much too painful for her to talk about. I think no one who lived through the Great Depression wants to talk about it. My mother was a young girl at the time. The events and the fear it generated shaped her life and, for a time, the national psyche.

My mother by her own account adored her father. He died when I was nineteen. I was mystified by an incident that occurred when my grandfather died.

"Janet," my grandmother called out desperately to my mother. "I can't believe it. I just can't believe your father is gone." My grandmother started to cry and reached out to hug my mother. It had only been a week since my grandfather's funeral. My grandmother was able to catch herself before she fell. You see, my mother had turned her back on my grandmother and simply walked away.

"He's gone, Mother," is all my mother said as she left the room. My mother always called my grandmother "Mother."

On one of our visits to my hometown I actually found some old photos of my mother when she was a child. "Why aren't you smiling in any of these photos?" I asked her.

"My mother said I had an ugly smile, so I shouldn't smile in any photos," she replied matter-of-factly. I recently found out that my maternal grandfather went to jail during the Depression for writing bad checks. I can't imagine how that must have affected my grandmother, mother, and uncle in the small Pennsylvania town they lived in. I don't think my grandmother ever forgave him for that.

My mother didn't like her own mother much. I suspect there were many good reasons for that in addition to her criticism of my mother's appearance. I think that's why my mother never liked me. I intuitively knew early on that my mother never liked me even though she never said anything. It took a lot longer for me to formally acknowledge it. When I did it was a relief. My mother has never told me she loved me even when I have said it to her. That seems like quite a record even for her stoic generation.

My dad would actually relate some stories from his childhood. His parents were divorced when he was a baby. That was 1927. His mother was pretty gutsy for that and a lot of other reasons. He was sent to live with his mother's sisters in a small town in western Pennsylvania. His aunt and uncle wanted to adopt him. His mother came one day from New York City where they lived and told her sister she was taking my dad on a train ride to the nearby city. She never brought him back. He was seven years old. He lived with his stepfather, mother, and two half siblings in various places in and around New York City. He attended four or five high schools in four or five years. He was sent away to military school several times.

As I matured I was able to glimpse more of what my parents were like outside the family and the close community we inhabited in my childhood. I would return to visit at least once a year for a week or two. They also would visit us one a year for extended stays. I knew they were very involved in the church after I was an adult just as they had been when

I was a child. However, they changed churches which, for my parents, was a huge decision. They joined an inner-city church which was located in a bad part of town. When I asked why, my dad said it was because that church was involved in ministering to the community, especially the homeless community surrounding it. I wouldn't realize until much, much later the scope of the compassionate work they were doing.

I realized that the generations who lived through the Great Depression—my grandparents, aunts, uncles, and parents—made community service an integral part of their lives. And it was not the community service of just giving money. They also gave of themselves, their time and talents. Their good deeds were never tainted with an attitude of blame or recrimination for the person they were helping. They gave back to the less fortunate regardless of the reason these people were needy. They don't see all they have as being earned or deserved by them because they worked hard, got an education, or any other reason. They see their fortune as luck, fate, or a gift from God. These generations had banded together to help each other through one of the most difficult times in the history of our country. They believed in the greater good of the community rather than the pathological individualism so prevalent in our country these days. They are grateful and appreciative for what they have been given. Yes, given. Not earned. The expressions I heard in my childhood so often, from my parents and grandparents and even in the larger community that I no longer hear now, like, "There but for the grace of God go I" or "To those to whom much is given much is required." I never heard them say as I hear so much now "you are entitled to," "you earned it," or "you deserve it." As I mused over that, I thought, "Maybe it is time for me to start being compassionate with my parents."

I suspect that my parents simply didn't know how to be supportive in the face of difficult life events like divorce, single parenting, and especially domestic violence. They learned to deal with the pain of their childhood by cutting themselves off from their emotions. That is a pattern the continued into their adult lives and a pattern that they taught me.

They structured their lives so they didn't have to face a great deal of change, emotional or otherwise. They especially avoided any huge life changing events. My dad worked for the same company for forty years.

They lived in the same city for sixty-plus years and only in two houses in all that time.

As with most things, I liked some things about such a predictable life, and I also found it stifling. It used to drive me crazy. I resented it because I knew how much the way they lived their lives had affected the choices I made. I didn't like being that predictable, that set in my ways. But that was the problem. I was thinking about them and evaluating them and their choices through the lens of my own life and desires. When I was able to begin to heal my childhood heartache, I was able to see them and their actions more objectively. I was able to put myself in their shoes and understand their pain. I could allow them to be who they were, without judgment or condemnation, and when that happened, I could begin to show them compassion. I was able to recognize that they did the best they could as parents, and I was able to be grateful for all they did give me spiritually, emotionally, and financially.

It was an eye-opening moment. If I could allow them to be themselves, and stop judging them as not being good parents or good enough, or not the, "the perfect parents," I could start viewing other people in my life in that way also. It was perfect timing because I was about to live through what was probably the most difficult time in my life. I would need all the compassion I could muster.

CHAPTER EIGHT

Love and Death Together

To say we fear the unknown is something of an understatement. Why do we have such a fear of the unknown? Why do we tend to torture ourselves with wild imaginings of what lies ahead? Have you ever noticed that our anxiety or dread of a future event is almost always worse than the actual event? In my experience, the fear surrounding the end of a relationship is usually much worse than the reality after it ends. But I have discovered that there is one exception to that general rule—a relationship ended by death.

"What's wrong with your arm?" I asked Brian. He had been moving his arm in circles and rubbing it for several minutes.

"It feels a little numb. I think it might be a pinched nerve," he replied. We had just completed our morning swim together. Brian and I carved out certain times to be alone together as a couple. That was something of a challenge as we had my three young children, full time and regular visits with his daughter, and another one on the way. We both worked at demanding jobs. In the summer time we would wake up early in the morning and swim laps together. We had a beautiful backyard and after swimming we would sit together for a brief time and talk over a cup of coffee. "It will probably go away on its own," Brian said to me. "If it doesn't, I will make an appointment with the doctor after the baby is born. It is probably a pinched nerve in my neck. I have already been through this once before with my back," Brian continued.

"I remember," I replied.

A couple of weeks after Brian first complained about his arm, our son Gary was born. Brian was ecstatic. He had always wanted a son. He was a rather macho guy. I didn't hold that against him. Being a mother again was exhilarating, and I was pleasantly surprised by that. For the past three years we had been working hard to blend our families. This baby accomplished in a moment what we had been unable to do in years. We all finally had a common bond or connection– a baby that we all loved and adored. I pinched myself to see if I was awake. Life was so great it had to be a dream.

"Did you see what he just did?" Ellen said to Bridget.

"Let me feed him! Let me change him! Let me push him in the stroller!" the two youngest girls would say as they fought over who could do things for Gary.

Samuel and Jessica were very involved as well. I often later would find one or several of the older children snuggled up on the couch with Gary watching a Disney movie. Everyone lingered at the dinner table to help feed him or to witness his latest accomplishment. Everyone wanted to go on family outings to the park to push Gary in the stroller or, later on, in the swing. The children all wanted to hang around the house in order to spend time with Gary. It helped that he was such a happy, fun baby. Suddenly these two separate camps had something in common. We all loved Gary.

Everyone, including myself, had anticipated Gary's arrival with some trepidation. Jessica was fifteen and was enormously embarrassed that I was pregnant. While I was pregnant she tried to keep me from having any contact with her schoolmates and friends. Everyone was wondering what changes it would bring to their life and place in the family. All of that simply washed away when Gary was brought home. Everyone wanted to hold him and help take care of him.

After Gary arrived, most of the tension melted away between Brian and my children and Bridget and all of us. Our love for Gary connected us. We really were becoming a family now—a group of people that genuinely loved and cared for each other. I don't think that bond would have developed without Gary. Bridget's weekend visits were even enjoyable. It was another set of hands to help with everything and Bridget seemed to enjoy helping and spending time with Gary. Through Gary we were sharing our lives and ourselves. I am sure there are other ways to create that bond other than having a baby. Maybe his arrival just sped up the process. We would need the love engendered by Gary's birth to get us through the trials we would be faced with shortly. Gary was the glue that held us all together. Without him I don't believe we would have survived as well as we did. I know I wouldn't have.

"Samuel, Jessica, Ellen, Bridget, can you all please come into the family room?" I yelled. Several different voices chimed in, asking why we wanted them all right then or asking if they could come in a few minutes. "No, we need everyone here right now," I said firmly. There was the sound of pounding feet or maybe it was just the pounding of my heart as Brian and I waited for everyone to arrive. Brian was seated in the middle of the sectional sofa. Samuel sat down right next to him. I don't remember where the girls sat. I was holding Gary in my arms. They were all looking at Brian eagerly waiting for him to announce plans for our next family vacation.

"I am going to die," Brian said. No one moved. No one made a sound. Even Gary was quiet in my arms. "I have a terminal illness. There is no treatment or cure. I don't know how long I have to live," Brian continued. Samuel's head was bowed, and he was quietly crying. I could see the tears dropping onto his shirt. I felt the tears on my face as I hugged Gary close to me. Should I let the children see me cry, I wondered. They are already losing one parent. If they see me cry, will they be afraid they are losing both parents? I didn't want them to think I didn't love Brian. On the other hand, I didn't want to make life more traumatic than it already was for them.

It was surreal how the routines of life pushed the illness into the background. They acted like a salve. But the knowledge of illness and death was always there, like a dark specter following you and haunting you everywhere you went. The only relief was sleep—at least some of the time.

You see, Brian had gone to visit the doctor as he promised. That night, as our two-week-old infant slept in his crib next to our bed, Brian told me the doctor thought he had ALS, commonly referred to as Lou

Gehrig's disease. They wanted to do more tests to be certain. I had never heard of ALS before. Brian gently explained to me what it was and told me that there was no treatment or cure. I was numb. Somehow I was able to sleep.

"How do you live with this pain every day? How do you get up every day and do the things that need to be done knowing that one of the persons you love most in the world is dying a little more each day that passes?" I asked Walt. He was the marriage counselor Brian and I had been going to see on and off for several years. I didn't really expect him to have an answer, although I secretly hoped he might have some small insight. Walt just looked at me with eyes that mirrored the despair in mine. He had no answers, not even any insights. This was unchartered territory. I would need, more than ever, to be compassionate as we all embarked on the arduous task of watching someone we love die a horrible and agonizing death. It would test the limits of my compassion for others. It would force me to discover my need for self-compassion. But it would also propel me to develop and practice compassion and self-compassion as an integral part of my daily life which practice has changed my life in ways I never imagined were possible.

The doctors provided the information regarding the physical progression of Brian's disease but they have absolutely no information regarding the emotional aspect. I felt like I was falling off a cliff with no safety net. There was no hope that Brian would survive, and I was starting to think there was no hope that I would survive either.

The demands of daily living came to my rescue. They numbed me to the pain. I felt like a zombie. I was physically present and functioning, but emotionally I was absent. My physical body or shell performed the daily tasks, but there was nothing inside.

Many years have passed, yet I still get overcome with emotion as I write this. I am both sad and angry—and everything in between—that I lost my husband to ALS. My emotions run the gauntlet. The past can still have a powerful hold over me at times.

When you lose someone, it is as if a piece has been ripped out of your heart, leaving a huge gaping hole. In the beginning the edges of the wound are shredded, torn, raw, and bleeding. The pain is excruciating and constant. Over time the wound begins to heal, but the hole remains. If you touch the hole you no longer experience a sharp, stabbing pain as you did when the wound was new. But the wound is still tender enough that a touch can bring tears to your eyes. The tender wound reminds me of the important lessons I learned from this horrendous experience. I am reminded to navigate life with compassion for myself and others. Compassion rescued from the depths of despair as I cared for Brian and afterwards. Compassion prevented me from becoming bitter and angry about my experience. It transformed tragedy into triumph.

"Get your affairs in order and prepare to die," the doctor said to Brian when he gave us the final diagnosis. "There is no treatment or cure. The average life span after the onset of symptoms is three years," the doctor continued. Brian asked some specific questions. Why is it that we often find comfort in knowledge? It is as if we believe a bunch of facts can change the outcome or ease the pain. I didn't really listen to the conversation between Brian and the doctor. I listened to the sound of Brian's voice thinking that I wouldn't be hearing that for much longer. I was startled back to what was happening when the doctor spoke the word "coffin."

"It is often called the coffin disease because you are trapped in a dead and lifeless body. The brain is never affected by the disease," the doctor continued.

Brian and I didn't explain all of this to the children when we called them into the family room or at any other time. The children weren't interested in details. I think it would have made things worse for them. They would have something else, in addition to death, to dread.

For the previous six months, our life had been a series of highs and lows as we lived through a myriad of medical tests that would confirm or maybe even reject that diagnosis. ALS is a cruel disease. The emotional devastation begins long before the physical deterioration manifests itself. It started as we waited for the confirmation of the initial diagnosis. At that time, the only way to diagnose ALS was by a process of elimination. If it didn't fit the pattern for other diseases, then it must by default be ALS. I think we were given the final diagnosis at Christmas, six months after Gary was born.

Right after the diagnosis, the best time for me was early in the morning when I was half awake. Initially, when I was waking up, I would have this ominous feeling in the pit of my stomach that something bad was going to happen. In my half-awake state, I could convince myself that the foreboding feeling was just the remnant of a very bad nightmare. But when I was fully awake I could no longer delude myself. As time went on, I would bolt awake with the feeling that I was going to throw up. It was a nightmare—just not the kind you have when you are asleep. Fortunately, whatever I was feeling could not be front and center for very long. There were many things to attend to, including a crying baby. However, this evil was never forgotten for long. It had taken up permanent residence in my psyche. It was like a black blot in my consciousness comprised of every horrible feeling you can imagine—pain, desperation, loneliness, rage, fear, anxiety. That black blot grew in size and shape as the disease progressed until at the end it almost swallowed me.

Tears would have been such a relief. I couldn't do it. I couldn't cry except on a very few occasions. And I wouldn't describe what I did then as crying. I emitted some kind of a primitive, primordial sound deep from within my body. It scared the hell out of me. I couldn't believe that sound came from me.

The first time it happened I was in the bathroom of our house. It was shortly after Brian told me about the disease. The last time was when I first saw Brian's lifeless body. I have no idea what brought it on the first time. I was alone in the house except for the baby who was sleeping. I collapsed onto the bathroom floor, screaming, crying, sobbing, heaving, writhing, and emitting that sound. I must have looked like some primitive animal that had been fatally shot and was slow to die.

Words were not coming out of my mouth only that weird, non-human sound. After several minutes I was exhausted. I lay on the floor quietly for a while, more exhausted than I had ever felt. I heard the baby cry. I slowly pulled myself up off the bathroom floor. It was time to get back to the demands of the living.

Brian first lost total use of his left arm. It just kind of hung on his body like a dead tree limb hangs from the trunk of a tree. When he walked it would flap around like a dead tree limb in the wind. Brian developed the habit, whenever he moved, of using his right arm to hold his left arm close to his body. His left arm would still hang loosely at his side when he held Gary with his right arm pressing him close to his chest. That left arm was a gruesome and constant reminder of the disease that was eating away at his body.

When I first met Brian, one of the things I found attractive about him was the way he dressed. I am not referring to the type of clothes that he wore. They were not expensive. But he was always neatly dressed. Perhaps the best way I can explain it was that Brian was in the military, and he continued many of those habits into his later life. His clothes were always neatly pressed, and he was always very well-groomed. He had beautiful hair. I know that is a strange thing to say about a man, but he did. One of the nurses even commented on it when he spent some time in hospice care. She described it as "U.S. Senator Hair." It was a beautiful gray color and very fine and soft.

Brian would wash and dry his hair each morning, comb it into place and then apply some hairspray. Well, the time inevitably came when Brian could no longer fix his own hair. This happened early on in the disease or as soon as he could no longer use his left arm. He had use of only one arm and you needed two to manage the hair dryer and the comb. He was still going to the office at that time. Brian was very particular about his appearance, especially his hair. It became my task to style his hair every morning. It was a huge process for me to try to get his hair to look like he did it. I could never do it right. He was usually disgusted with me. Disgusted may be too tame an adjective, but I will leave it at that.

After I dried and styled Brian's hair, I would dress him. That was a bit easier at least at that point in time. Brian's balance was impaired but he was still able to steady himself on a counter or wall while standing. Once he was fairly steady he would lift each leg and I would put his pant leg over his foot. Unfortunately, each day brought many more and new aggravations and limitations.

"You b****. You whore. You are so stupid. How can anyone be as stupid as you are? F*** you! You are a piece of s***!" Brian shrieked at me. Brian was staring at me and his entire face was contorted with rage and hatred. "Get the f*** out of here!" he screamed at me. I had just raised my head up from the floor where I had been putting on Brian's slacks. My hands are trembling as I write this. I felt something brush against my head after I bent down. I realized that Brian had taken a swing at me with the fist of his good arm. He missed me because I had ducked down to put on his pants. It took me a minute to sort all this out. I was stunned. The look on Brian's face was terrifying. It was beyond rage. "Get the f*** out of here!" he kept screaming at me.

I was shaking as I left the room. "Close the f****** door on your way out, you b****!" he screamed at me. I left the bedroom and closed the door. My whole body was shaking. I felt like I was going to throw up. I waited a little while and then I knocked on the door. "Get away from that f****** door," Brian screamed from inside the room. I ran to the telephone and called one of his friends.

"Richard, I don't know what to do. Brian is in the bedroom and refuses to come out. He is acting irrationally. Can you come over?" I asked. I didn't tell Richard about anything that had happened. To his credit Richard came right over to the house. Richard knocked at the bedroom door and announced his presence. I heard Brian tell him to come in. I have no idea what was said between them that morning. Richard left after about an hour. I went in and helped Brian get dressed. We didn't speak. Brian left for the office shortly thereafter.

I was still shaking after Brian left. I was angry to say the least. Rage would be a better term. I was going over scenarios of what I would do or say to him when he got home or, God forbid, the next time this happened. After I ranted and raved for a while, I finally calmed down. My rage was spent. I started to remember my love for Brian and how he was enduring unimaginable emotional pain. I asked myself, "How do I know how I would act if I was the one dying a horrible and agonizing death?"

If I had to pinpoint the one moment where I had made the conscious decision to look beyond myself, I think it was then. When I asked myself that simple, age-old question of "How would I feel if I were in his shoes?" The seeds of compassion were being planted. Brian and I never spoke about the events of that day.

Brian's walk became increasingly unsteady. He would teeter and totter when he walked, and I was terrified he would fall down. He started using a cane to steady himself. He couldn't use that for very long because he couldn't hold it when he lost the use of his right arm. I bought a wheelchair and put it in the family room hoping he would use it. It sat there empty for quite a while. Brian was having difficulty standing for any extended period of time. He was becoming fatigued very easily. One night we had a few of his high school friends over. He grabbed the wheelchair and sat in it. He was able to move around to talk to everyone that way. It still sat there empty for a while after that.

"Do you want to rent a wheelchair for the day?" I asked Brian. He just ignored me and my request. I didn't say anything else because I knew it was useless to do so. We started walking through the zoo. Brian started to get very tired. He found a bench to sit down. Without asking him I went back to the entrance and rented a wheelchair for the day. I arrived back at the bench with the wheelchair. Brian didn't say anything. He just got into the wheelchair. He looked haggard and defeated. Brian refused to look at me for the remainder of our day at the zoo. He seemed to feel a little better when Gary asked to ride on his lap. As a toddler Gary thought it was great fun.

Around that same time, Brian stopped being able to drive himself to the office, so one of the employees at the company, Clark, would come to pick him up every day. Clark would put Brian and the wheelchair in the car. When they arrived at the office Clark would put Brian in the wheelchair and arrange his arms on his lap. If he didn't do this carefully the arms would dangle and flap around and get caught in the wheels. Brian would sit in the wheelchair in his office. He didn't have the ability to move the wheelchair. What a blessing the day I discovered that we could get him an electric wheel chair. For a while, he had enough use of his right thumb that he could push the lever to control the chair. But by the time he lost the use of this thumb, he had already stopped going into the office.

The phone rang. I picked it up. "This is Officer Smith of the police department. We would like you to come to the police station tomorrow at ten o'clock a.m. to talk to us about your son, Samuel."

"Okay," I responded. I hung up the phone.

"Who is it?" Brian asked.

I lied. "It was nothing important," I said.

Brian accepted that answer. If he weren't sick, he would have known I was lying. This was the first of many such calls. We soldiered on.

"I have to go to the bathroom," Brian said. He wasn't able to physically shake me to wake me up at this point in time.

"Okay," I said. "Just give me a minute to wake up."

"I have to go right now!" Brian said desperately. Patience was never one of Brian's virtues, but who knows for how long he had been trying to wake me. His voice was not very strong at this point in time, and I was in an exhausted state of sleep. I walked to his side of the bed. I wrapped my arms around his waist and hoisted him to his feet. He steadied himself for a minute. "Okay," he said to me. We started to walk very slowly to the bathroom. Brian held onto my arm as he shuffled his feet. I lowered him onto the toilet seat. After he was done, I leaned him against my body as I reached around to wipe him. I pulled his bottoms back up. (We had actually done this in an airplane bathroom on several occasions. That could be the subject matter of a comedy skit). We proceeded slowly back to the bed. Just before we reached the bed, Brian lost his balance and fell to the floor with a resounding thud.

"Help, help!" Brian desperately pleaded. I was frantically pulling and tugging to try to get him on his feet. It was the middle of the night. Last time this happened my father had been around to help. He wasn't here now.

"I'm going to have to wake up Samuel," I said to Brian.

"Please don't," he pleaded.

"I have to. I can't get you off the floor," I said. I rolled Brian over onto his back and put a pillow under his head. I went to get Samuel. Samuel and I managed to pull Brian off the floor in increments using a small stool and to get him back into the bed. Brian would fall a few more times before he finally agreed to use the wheelchair all the time.

"I really need a break," I said one morning to Brian. "I would like someone to come and help for four hours a day a couple of times a week."

"No," Brian responded, and by the look in his eyes I knew he meant it. That was not the first time I had said this or the first time Brian rejected my request. Brian would not allow anyone but me to do anything for him. That is not to say that there were a lot of offers of help but there were a few. He would stay alone with his daughter, Bridget, but that was awfully hard on her. She was about twelve years old. If I did leave them to take the other children someplace or go to the grocery store, I would be sure to take Brian to the bathroom before I left and to arrive back before he had to make another trip. Usually he and his daughter sat in the family room and watched TV while I was gone. That was the extent of the help he would accept. Brian even refused to allow his sister, Nancy, to stay with him so I could go to the store. I understood his reasons, and I honored his wishes for as long as I could.

I really didn't want any of the children to have to do any unpleasant things for Brian. Sometimes Brian couldn't wait for me to finish doing something so one of the children would feed him. They had such a look of distress on their face when they were doing that. Brian started having difficulty swallowing his food. We stopped eating dinner together after he almost choked at the dinner table a couple of times. We had some type of a suction apparatus to use when he got something stuck in his throat.

"Brian, this is Susan. She is going to stay with you while I go to the grocery store," I said. I was surprised that Susan agreed to stay after seeing the look of hatred and rage Brian gave both of us. After his time with the nurses' aide concluded, Brian would complain about her for hours.

"You know she is going to drop me. She isn't strong enough. I am going to get really hurt when she drops me," Brian said when I arrived home. Brian insisted on getting a shower every morning. That didn't fit with the hospice schedule. Hospice would send someone to shower him, but it would have to be in the afternoon and not daily. Brian wouldn't agree to wait, so I showered him every morning. I tried to turn that duty over to the nurse's aide one day of the week. It was worth it to put up with Brian's complaining and looks of hatred to have a brief respite. Eventually Brian would have worn me down and I would have stopped using the nurse's aide. It never came to that because not long thereafter Brian ended up at a hospice in patient facility.

The disease ate away at and ravaged our emotions just as it ate away at and ravaged Brian's body. Adversity by its nature is unique. We each define it differently and we each cope with it in our own way. Occasionally I would hear a story of other widows and widowers and it would give me hope that I could survive but it really didn't give me the tools to get through each and every day. I didn't want to go about my business as usual pretending everything was fine. Yet what was the alternative? I had to find my own way to live with the pain just like I would eventually have to find my own way to heal. I felt like I was slowing sinking into a quicksand of despair. No one seemed to be able to throw me a lifeline. Certainly Brian could not.

We seek and crave connections but we often feel alone, especially in our darkest hours. No one is experiencing what we are experiencing. We are isolated in our despair. Only those who are also experiencing it can understand it and share the burden and pain. Brian was the one person who shared the experience with me. But he was enveloped in his own dark world of fear and despair. Physically, Lou Gehrig's disease deprived Brian of the ability to reach out and touch me. Emotionally, it rendered him incapable of reaching out and connecting with me. I lost him the minute the diagnosis was given. Our emotional connection was severed when the death sentence was pronounced. I didn't realize that at the time. I so wanted to connect with him, to grow even closer to him for whatever time he had left. But wishing doesn't make it so. What is that old expression? "If wishes were horses, beggars would ride." Brian was entirely wrapped up in his own world—a maze of fear, anxiety, regrets, physical pain, anger, remorse, and hatred.

All that remained was the memory of our great love. That memory would have to sustain us for the few remaining years. I was reminded of a car rambling down the last distance of road on the fumes from its once-full gas tank. Our lives were reduced to waiting for the end to come and trying to manage the final journey as gracefully as possible. It was about wheelchairs, bedpans, feeding tubes, bedsores, insomnia, assisted showers, assisted trips to the bathroom, and containing the rage and fear. His pain was my pain and so we traveled down that long, dark road to death together but apart.

We were separated by a wall of silence and anger—his and mine. I tried to talk to Brian about how I felt. I often asked how he felt. He was silent. He would look at me with eyes filled with anger and hatred. I suppose he thought it should have been obvious to me how he felt. And I was angry with him for pushing me away and for a lot of other reasons including how he treated me as I struggled to care for him. I was resentful of his ever-increasing demands and the burden he placed on me and the family.

"You need to be civil to me," I said angrily. "I am not going to do anything else for you until you agree to be civil to me!" I exclaimed. "I can't take being called names, struck at, or cursed at any longer!" Brian's outbursts had become much more frequent. I knew from the few ALS support group meetings that I attended that this behavior was not unique to Brian, but that didn't make it much easier to bear. When I said this to him, Brian was sitting in his lift chair in the family room watching TV. He ignored me. I returned to the kitchen where Gary was helping me with dinner. A little while later I heard Brian call my name several times. His voice was getting weaker at this point, and I think at first he wasn't sure if I had actually heard him. By this time Gary was hanging out with one of his siblings in their room. "I am not going to help you with anything until you tell me you are going to stop calling me names and cursing at me!" I repeated.

"I have to go to the bathroom," he demanded.

I walked into the family room. "I'm not going to take you to the bathroom. I already told you that I am not going to do anything else for you unless you agree to start treating me better. I will be happy to call someone else to help you if you want me to," I said firmly. Brian just stared at me again with a look of rage and hatred. I imagine the need to urinate was becoming urgent, and he finally realized that I was going to let him piss in his pants unless he agreed to stop trying to hit me and stopped cursing at me and calling me names. I was at my wit's end with him.

"Call James for me," Brian demanded.

I dialed the phone and held it up to Brian's ear. "Can you come and pick me up?" I heard him ask James. A short time later the doorbell rang. I answered the door and escorted James into the family room where Brian was seated. James looked very confused.

"If Brian wants to say right now that he will stop mistreating me, I will be glad to help him go to the bathroom," I said to James in front of Brian.

"Let's go," Brian said to James. James looked pretty scared. James had some experience with helping Brian. He would assist Brian to go to the bathroom on occasion at the office. James didn't say anything. He had known and worked with Brian for many, many years. They left to go to James' house. This was a hard thing for me to do on many levels. I wanted to be the loving caregiver in my eyes, Brian's eyes and the eyes of the world. The action I was taking definitely did not fit that image, but I was about to collapse emotionally and physically. That was my litmus test—if it came to the point I could no longer function, I needed to change something. This was one of those times. I had reached my limit, and I needed to honor that and practice some self-compassion. I felt selfish doing this, but there are limits to everything—including compassion I have learned. Compassion does not require us to ignore all of our own needs while being compassionate to another.

"Brian wants to come home," James said to me over the phone an hour or so later.

"Okay, as long as he knows the conditions under which I will take care of him," I replied.

"He does," James said. Brian arrived home. He and I never discussed anything about that day. Brian never apologized or even acknowledged that he mistreated me. Brian was still difficult, to say the least, but the (attempted) hitting and cursing stopped

I repeated my mantra, "How do I know how I would act if I was the one dying a horrible and agonizing death?" I didn't want to judge him. I just wanted the abuse to stop. It took me a while to realize that I had a right to set some standards for acceptable behavior from Brian.

Eventually I stopped trying to connect with Brian. I think Brian remained angry until the day he died. I recently read that a person dies in the same way that he lived. Brian was, in many ways, always a person filled with anger. I couldn't control how he chose to die. I could only control how I chose to react to him and the situation. My anger over his refusal or inability to connect faded. I reminded myself that I had no right to judge him. I had no right to presume I would handle it any differently or any better than Brian was handling it. There was no right way to handle this, at least none that I know of. How arrogant of me to presume that there was. When I would become exasperated or impatient or angry with him I would ask myself that one simple question again, "How do I know how I would act if I was the one dying a horrible and agonizing death?"

I don't know how many thousands of times I asked myself that, but it was my lifeline. It represents a true moment of compassion, and it illustrates just how deeply a moment of compassion can affect you and those around you. I understood the power of that question and how it helped me cope with caring for Brian. But I was able to see so much more after he died and I had some time to reflect and process what I had experienced. Compassion begins, does it not, with that question? If we honestly put ourselves in the other person's shoes, we can no longer judge them because we experience what they are experiencing. We understand on some level their fear, anxiety, anger, and more. We respond with love and caring wanting to treat that person the way we would want to be treated if we were in his/her shoes.

My love for Brian had changed. Somewhere along the way in dealing with this disease, my deep love for Brian had turned into devotion and compassion. But even compassion for others and devotion to them have their limits, I had learned. As I look back on that incident I realize that when I set those limits on Brian I was practicing a form of tough love. If someone is treating you badly, and you're doing your very best to help them, then it's okay to set boundaries, sometimes really hard ones.

I felt very guilty about my behavior at the time. Compassion encompasses being kind, caring, helpful, thoughtful, and more, but it does not include being taken advantage of or even abused. Setting limits is a form of self-compassion and something I have struggled to do all my life. I am still learning how to do that.

You don't have to put the other person's needs ahead of your own all the time. I think we women are especially vulnerable to this. We often feel and act as if our needs and wants are not as important as those of others because perhaps we are not as important. Some of it is an issue of self-esteem, I think. But also our culture tells us that if we are not caring, nurturing and giving all the time we are not a good wife, mother, friend, neighbor, co-worker etc. In some ways, our self-worth is based on taking care of and doing for others. It is a powerful message to overcome.

Before the illness, Brian was one of the most energetic people I ever knew. He reminded me of the Energizer Bunny in that old TV commercial. He ran his own business. He attended a multitude of sporting events, social events, and business events. He did all kinds of projects around the house. After we were married he cooked, cleaned, and spent time with the children at home and with them at their extracurricular activities. He had his regular visits with his own daughter—driving to pick her up and take her home several times a week. He was always moving. I rarely saw him sit down and relax.

"What do you want to watch today?" I asked Brian. He turned to me with a look of disgust on his face. I tried to find something that would interest him. It was daytime TV after all, and this was before the proliferation of cable networks. The pickings were slim. I settled him into his lift chair located in the corner of the family room. He would sit there and watch TV until it was time to go to bed. Occasionally we had an outing, but it was very rare. At this stage in his illness, he was not really interested in going anywhere. I think it was physically tiring for him, but it was also embarrassing as people stared at him. As I settled him into his chair, I was reminded of one of our last outings with Brian.

"What do you mean, you are out of minivans?" I shrieked at the poor man at the rental car counter. "I made this reservation over a month ago. I have to have a minivan. My husband is handicapped, and I can't get him in and out of any other vehicle. I am begging you to please find us a minivan," I continued. As I said this I waved in the direction of the family seated on the floor to the right of the rental counter. Brian was sitting in his wheelchair and the four older children were seated in the midst of our luggage for six people and a baby, portable crib, car seat, electric wheelchair battery, and stroller. One-year-old Gary was seated on Samuel's lap. Needless to say, we looked like a group of displaced persons.

We eventually got our minivan. When we arrived at our hotel, I barked out directions to the children like a military officer. "Samuel and Jessica, you are in charge of the luggage, portable crib, and electric wheelchair battery. Bridget, you are in charge of Gary. Ellen, you will take and set up the stroller for Gary. We can leave the car seat in the minivan. I will set up the electric wheelchair and get Brian into it. Does everyone know what to do?" I asked. Everyone said they did. I will never forget the look of amazement on the face of the valet parking attendant at the hotel as we unloaded ourselves, the luggage, and equipment from the minivan. We were going back to visit Brian's hometown. This was the last trip we ever took together

"Can you come downstairs and scratch my nose?" I vaguely heard Brian say over the baby monitor. To this day I can't hear the static of a baby monitor without feeling depressed. After a prolonged period of sleepless nights, I started going upstairs to the bedroom to lie down when Gary was taking his nap. I would turn on the baby monitor that I had set up next to Brian's lift chair and the one I had next to me in the bedroom. I rarely got a chance to rest, much less sleep. As soon as my head would touch the pillow, I would hear Brian's voice over the monitor. "Can you come downstairs? I need you to rearrange my arm," or "Can you come downstairs? I need you to change the TV station," or "Can you come downstairs? I need you to…"

Sometimes I would simply turn off the monitor and open the bedroom door so I could hear if anything serious happened. I couldn't sleep, but at least I could rest. Brian's voice was soft, but I could still hear him call me.

"Why didn't you come downstairs when I called you?" Brian would ask on the days I turned the monitor off.

"I didn't hear you," I would lie. Of course he knew I was lying. I felt so awful about myself at the time. I would tell myself what a terrible person I was to ignore the needs of a terminally ill and almost totally helpless person. But I had to have a break from the constant demands if I was going to retain my sanity.

The pull between compassion and self-compassion was a daily struggle, and I always felt terribly guilty if I didn't put Brian first all the time. It was not until sometime after he died that I was able to forgive myself, another act of self-compassion, for not being the perfect caregiver. Insomnia is a by-product of this disease. So Brian didn't sleep and that meant I didn't sleep. He would sleep a little. As the months went by, the nights and days blurred. It is impossible to describe the level of exhaustion—physically, spiritually, and emotionally. Numbness was my friend. Brian would sleep in fits and starts. I would be jolted awake by, "I need you to turn me over," or "I need you to scratch my leg," or "I need you to rearrange my arms." I didn't have the energy to put him in the wheelchair at night to take him to the bathroom, so we used a urinal in the bed. Often after Brian would use the urinal I would find myself lying in a wet spot. I didn't care. I just wanted to get a few minutes of sleep.

I cry as I write this. It is almost twenty years since Brian's death and yet the wound still seeps and oozes. Am I still grieving? Maybe. It is more likely that the memories of intense emotional pain live on in our psyche like memories of intense physical pain. Something touches the wound and it begins to ooze and seep. The specific event that triggers the oozing and seeping is a mystery. I fully expected that birthdays, anniversaries, and special events would trigger that reaction. I got through those days fine. It was the unexpected little events that triggered it. In the beginning the phone would ring and I would run to it expecting to hear, "Hi, honey." Now it usually happens when I see our son, a young man now, doing something I am so proud of, and I want to share it with Brian.

His face was contorted, his eyes were wide and he was flailing, at least with his eyes. Funny how Brian's body language was so limited, but I could read just about everything in his face and his eyes. His eyes were moving rapidly in all directions, imitating the flailing of limbs. I had come into the room in response to some commotion I had heard. "Take me outside, take me outside NOW!" Brian kept saying in the loudest voice he could muster—a mere whisper. I put him in the wheelchair and took him outside. I called for my oldest daughter, Jessica, to sit with him while I called the doctor's office to see if I needed to take him to the emergency room. I didn't want Brian to hear me discussing him with the doctor.

"I will call in a prescription," the nurse said to me.

"What is the prescription for?" I asked.

"The prescription is for anxiety," she said compassionately.

"Should I take him to the emergency room?" I asked the nurse.

"No, there is nothing physically wrong with him. This should be all he needs," she replied. I went back outside to see how my daughter and Brian were doing.

"I am going to die," I heard Brian say to Jessica, my oldest daughter. That was the first and last time I ever heard him say that. I wheeled him back into the house after a little while. Anti-anxiety drugs became a daily part of his life.

Some time later Brian became ill with an upper respiratory illness or so we thought. We took him to a hospice facility. We didn't think he would recover but, after a few months, Brian unexpectedly recovered enough to return home. He was, by then, totally bedridden. He was able to come home because his company generously agreed to pay for caregivers. "Thank you so much for your generosity," I said to John one day. He was Brian's business partner.

"I am glad to do it even though, if the roles were reversed, I don't believe Brian would do it for me," John replied. I understood what John said, and there was an element of truth to it for both John and I. John made it possible for us to have two caregivers—one person for twelve hours during the day and another for a twelve-hour night shift. The hospice nurse was also coming on a regular basis after Brian returned home.

"Brian is still in a lot of pain. We need to check his urine. He shouldn't be experiencing that much pain with the amount of morphine he is taking," the hospice nurse told us during one of her regular visits.

"This disease is a particularly cruel one," I remember thinking. The afflicted person can't move his/her limbs but he/she has full sensations or feeling in his/her body. They can be in a great deal of pain.

Tony, our day-time caregiver, threw a fit. Brian had a catheter so it wouldn't be difficult to obtain the urine for testing. I couldn't understand Tony's resistance to the request. Tony and I got into a heated argument. "I will quit if I have to do that!" Tony finally shouted.

"Then quit," I said. "The nurse says we need to do this for Brian, so we will!" I shouted. The hospice nurse was silent during this exchange, but she never followed up on the request. Maybe she knew what Nancy, Brian's sister, apparently already knew. Tony was stealing Brian's morphine. He was a drug addict. I was apparently the only one who didn't know this.

After Brian died, Nancy told me about Tony. "We didn't want to add to your burdens," Nancy explained when I asked why she hadn't told me earlier. That would explain a lot of things like the disappearance of items of value from the house and the fact that Tony was often late for work.

Sela, our night person, would wait patiently for Tony to arrive even though it made her children late for school. I told her I could manage for a while without any help. Maybe she didn't believe me. I think rather she had so much compassion for Brian and I that she didn't want to abandon us in our hour of need. Sela just oozed love, patience and compassion in all of her dealings with Brian and with me. She was a saint.

Would it have been better to have known about Tony earlier? Maybe it would have helped me recognize the signs of drug use in my children. I had no idea what the signs of drug use were. Maybe I could have prevented the loss of some of those sentimental items.

"Tony took good care of Brian," Nancy said. She was right, and that is really what mattered at the time.

For a while I think Brian believed he was going to defeat the disease by sheer willpower. He was going to will himself to live. He had so much to live for. He had always wanted a son. Now he had one. He had always wanted a family. Now he had one.

Against his doctor's wishes and without his knowledge, we tried all types of alternative therapies. I know that one of the therapies actually stopped the progression of the disease. But Brian wanted more. He wanted to be cured. I guess this is greed of a different sort. I argued with him to continue the treatment. But he never went back for that alternative treatment. I accepted his decision. I think part of dealing with a terminally ill person is letting them have control over those aspects of their life they can still control. The disease had not affected his brain.

"Could you do it?" Brian asked me long before the final diagnosis was made. He never said what "it" was, but I knew what he meant or at least I thought I did. I said I didn't know, but I was going to expect the best from myself. You see, I was referring to being able to take care of a terminally ill spouse. Brian was referring to assisted suicide.

"Please don't ask me to do that," I begged. He never mentioned it to me again. Instead he summoned one of his closest friends to the house. They talked behind closed doors. I knew Brian asked him if he would do it. I know his friend said yes only because I saw the look of relief in Brian's eyes after his friend left.

This friend never came to visit Brian the entire time he was sick. But somehow the commitment his friend made that day comforted Brian throughout this ordeal. Maybe he just wanted to feel he still had some control over his life or maybe he wanted to know the suffering could be ended when he couldn't bear it anymore. He knew he would be physically incapable of doing it himself. I often wondered if I let him down. But how do you kill someone that you love? That is not a decision I wanted to be faced with. After that conversation Brian and I never again spoke about his death. We never shared our feelings of what we were going through. Brian was a pretty macho guy. I guess I can be macho too. We just soldiered on.

If only if it played out like it did in the old movies. The sick person becomes immersed in love and wants only to connect with and ease the inevitable loss and suffering of his loved ones. I can't remember any of the names of those movies but there were many such heroines who were in wheelchairs or dying. They thought only of the suffering of their loved ones. We viewers wanted to be like them, and of course we inevitably failed. Today we have reality TV. We measure ourselves by the lowest common denominator of human behavior now. I wonder if this reality stuff is any better for us than the creation of a perfect image. It seems to have given us permission to stop striving to be a better person or to act nobly. Of course, Brian didn't emulate the perfect behavior of the terminally ill heroes of the old movies and neither did I. I was certainly not always compassionate or caring. I never said anything, but I often felt overburdened and resentful. I tried to hide it, but I'm sure I wasn't always successful. We didn't celebrate our basest behavior either. I strived to meet the ideal of the ever patient, attentive, compassionate and loving caregiver even though I knew I would fail. Isn't that the way it should be?

Brian was totally bedridden for the last five months of his life. He stayed in another part of the house. His caregiver would wheel him into the family room, but that happened less and less. Later, the caregiver would open the blinds in Brian's bedroom so he could watch Gary and I play in the back yard. I would pop into Brian's room often during the day. At night Brian and I would watch a TV program together. The misery and suffering dragged on, seeming at times to be endless. Brian elected to get a feeding tube, but he remained steadfast in his decision not to use a respirator. I have to admit I was thankful for that.

"It is ten o'clock, and Brian is still asleep. What should I do?" asked the weekend caregiver. I went into Brian's room to check on him again. He was sleeping peacefully. I checked to make sure he was breathing. He was.

"Let him sleep a while longer," I said. "He was awake unusually late last night and must be very tired. Remember that I am going out for a few hours this afternoon," I told the caregiver. I was taking an outing other than my usual trip to the grocery store or to attend the children's activities. The Russian ballet was in town performing Swan Lake. I was so looking forward to the performance.

I am not particularly knowledgeable about ballet. I just enjoy it. I have always loved the scene in *Swan Lake* called "Dance of the Swans." I have always found the music, the imagery, and gracefulness beautiful and peaceful. This performance was no exception. I was totally immersed in the scene. On the stage, the ballerinas fluttered their arms gracefully upward. I saw their entire bodies floating upward, not just their arms. They were angels ascending into heaven. As I watched I had a feeling of intense peacefulness and contentment. I was totally drawn into the image on the stage. I became part of it. I was disconnected from time and place.

The curtain fell for intermission. I often wondered what the dire circumstances were that necessitated someone being paged over the PA system at a large venue. Now I know. Suddenly I heard my name announced over the PA system. The feeling of peace and contentment vanished with the sound of my name. I already knew. As I rushed home I felt scared, apprehensive, relieved, and guilty, but mostly I just felt numb.

The room was exactly as I had left it just an hour or so earlier. Brian was resting peacefully on the bed. It was only on very close examination you could detect that Brian's chest was not moving. I had known for three years that this day would come. It was inevitable. The day the doctor gave that diagnosis almost three years ago was the same day Brian and I received our death sentence. We knew that his life—our relationship, our life together, our job as co-parents and our world would end much sooner than we expected. On this beautiful sunny Sunday afternoon, Brian had simply stopped breathing.

I reached out and touched Brian's hand. It felt like a stone on a cold winter night. I felt my body shudder. I remember being amazed that life could depart so quickly. I dropped to my knees and laid my head on my knees. Then I heard that horrible sound again, the primitive wailing. It definitely was not human. I looked up. I looked around the room. I was alone. I realized it was coming from me! I continued to wail while I rocked back and forth on my knees. I remember thinking it was strange that I wasn't shedding any tears. I have no idea how much time I passed like that. When I was spent, I got up, kissed Brian, and left the room.

My remorse at not being at his side when he stopped breathing was short-lived. We had been together at the moment of his death. Brian died during the "Dance of the Swans," or maybe it was angels. As I left the room I again felt the peace that I had experienced during the ballet performance.

After Brian died and the nightmare of caring for a terminally ill person was over, I was able to take a step back and reflect, and what I saw amazed me. I eventually realized that compassion had bound us together in inexplicable ways and created a connection between us that was deeper than I could have ever imagined. It was not created by words. Brian and I never spoke about his illness after the initial diagnosis. We never spoke about how we would, should or were handling his death. We really never talked for almost three years about anything other than his asking and demanding that I take care of his physical needs.

Still the trials of going through this event together joined us together in a way that even sharing our most intimate thoughts and desires never could have. I felt an unspoken connection of love and devotion that was created by my compassion for Brian. Brian remained angry and full of rage throughout his ordeal. Still, I know on some level Brian was grateful for what I did even if he did not express it. Often the person in pain cannot express their appreciation or thanks. They are overwhelmed by their own pain. It is a bit akin to the way parents know their children, especially teenagers, still love them even when they are angry with them and act hatefully toward them. Brian's failure to show me compassion was not an impediment to my experiencing the magic of compassion. Compassion does not have to be reciprocated to be practiced. Compassion is freely given without judgment and without expecting anything in return. It benefits the giver as much, if not more, than the receiver. The fact that Brian was not compassionate in return did not prevent compassion from transforming my life and me. Without compassion I never could have been devoted to Brian and cared for him as I did. We would have continued as we started out, arguing and being resentful. I would have placed him in a nursing home while I anxiously waited for him to die to escape the burden. Everything changed when I saw him and our life together with compassion. I felt an incredible connection to Brian through my acts of compassion.

Compassion takes us out of our selfish selves—if only we let it in. We don't feel superior, morally or otherwise, when we feel compassion for another. We don't feel anger toward the person to whom we are showing compassion. I didn't feel I was a better person than Brian because I was compassionate when he was full of rage. If you are feeling superior, you are not being compassionate. There is no superiority in compassion just common humanity and suffering. Compassion is a great equalizer.

Compassion has the power to transform our life and the lives of others. It can grow and flourish even when the person to whom you are showing compassion is angry and hateful. I can't explain it other than to say compassion is magic.

Compassion transformed the agonizing experience of watching my beloved husband die from Lou Gehrig's disease into an experience of unparalleled love and connection. After all I had been through with Brian's illness, I was amazed to discover that there was still so much more to learn about compassion. I would learn so much more about compassion as I dealt with the devastation the disease and death had on our family.

CHAPTER NINE

The Aftermath of Death

FOR THE FIRST YEAR AFTER BRIAN DIED, I WAS LIVING IN TWO WORLDS. The only place I wanted to be was in the past reliving my life with Brian. But life and its ever pressing demands forced me to live in the present as well. Outside events and my emotions were spiraling out of control and this was one of the darkest times in my life. In retrospect, I realize that this was also the time in my life when I learned the most about overcoming tragedy, living a meaningful and connected life, and the role of compassion in learning those lessons. It was a time of inexplicable pain and monumental personal growth. I am so grateful I had the opportunity to learn those lessons no matter how difficult the circumstances were.

When we first met, Brian and I felt a glimmer of a connection. It initially appeared only in rare moments. We built on those rare moments. We forged stronger and more lasting connections through sharing the joys and trials of our life together. The connections that bound Brian and I together were forged from sharing events like the death of his mother, the illness and death of his father, the challenges and joys of raising four children, the birth of our son, enjoying trips together and with friends, sharing the burdens of the physical demands of daily living, and facing a terminal illness and death. Those individual, separate connections eventually formed an unbroken chain. The chain grew stronger with the addition of each new link. It grew so strong it could be broken only by death. The connection could never even begin to form without love—the type of love that caused us to commit to each other. By commit, I don't mean marriage. I mean commit to change ourselves and our lives to make the relationship work and flourish. Setting limits and demanding that the life we forge together meets some of our own needs is part of the commitment we make to ourselves. We can't subjugate all of our needs and wants to those of our partner. That is the self-compassion component of relationships.

Love can't be rushed, or maybe I should say the recognition of love takes time. We have to allow the time to eliminate the many false loves that seek to deceive us. A relationship has to be a give-and-take. We can't be so desperate for a relationship that we compromise what we want and who we are. If genuine love is at the core of a relationship, then the give-and-take will flow. One partner may give more than the other at times but the give and talk will ultimately balance itself out.

There is no magic formula for creating a healthy, fulfilling relationship. Love it the key ingredient but it is a mystery what creates and sustains that love. It is not a mystery what can destroy that love.

I had seen Brian at his worst. He had seen me at my worst. We had said and done terrible things to each other. Sometimes it seems like it was almost a contest to see who could be crueler. Brian punished with words. I punished with silence. We brought out the worst and the best in each other. We experienced together every day events and catastrophic events. We shared a history. We shared our lives. Through it all I still loved Brian. Through it all he still loved me. We knew each other with all our warts and yet we still loved each other. That is a true love story, isn't it?

"Can you come over tomorrow and help me clean out the garage and Brian's sickroom?" I asked Tony, Brian's former caregiver a few weeks after Brian died. Tony agreed to help.

Brian was something of a pack rat, so the garage and bedroom were filled with boxes and boxes of paper, documents, and other stuff. Brian had closed out a storage unit and put everything in the garage and the extra bedroom he eventually occupied. He never got a chance to sort through it.

Tony started in the garage and I started in the bedroom. Some of the boxes in the bedroom were ones that had been delivered to us from

Brian's office after he stopped going there. Brian didn't seem interested in looking through them, so I had simply put them into the closet. They sat there unopened for many, many months.

I pulled the first box out. It contained all sorts of outdated papers from Brian's business. I went and got a huge trash bin and started throwing things away. After sifting through three or four boxes I came to one that contained some photographs. I set them aside to look at later after I had gone through all the boxes.

I decided to take a break. Looking through these documents was akin to sifting through parts of Brian's life, and it was very difficult. It was painful. So I was looking forward to savoring the photos of Brian and I together in happier times. I grabbed the photos and went into the kitchen to get a cup of coffee. I would browse through the photos leisurely. I was concerned that the photos would bring up some painful memories, and I wanted to be prepared when they did. I steeled myself and opened the first envelope. It contained photos of Brian and Bridget on a trip. It looked like a trip to Disneyland. I could see Cinderella's castle in the background of the photo.

As I looked through the photos I tried to remember when Brian and I had taken a trip to Disneyland with the children. With all that had transpired over the last three years of caring for Brian, my memory was a bit sketchy. I looked at the date stamped on the photos to help me figure this out. At the time the photos were taken, we were definitely married and had been for several years. I looked through a few more photos trying to remember this trip. Then I saw her. I recognized Kendra right away. She was the former girlfriend of one of our mutual friends. In several of the photos she and Brian had their arms wrapped around each other. There were several envelopes full of photos of Brian and Kendra together. In some of the photos, they were kissing each other. I had just spent three years of my life caring for my husband under the most difficult of circumstances. Now just a few weeks after he died I discovered that he had an affair while we were married. As I stared at the photos with tears streaming down my face and anger welling up in my throat, I tried to think clearly. Did this trip take place during the brief period of time Brian and I were separated? Maybe, but if it did, he never told me about it when we got back together. I have to find out now after he is dead, and I can't angrily confront him about it.

Compassion may be the key ingredient in a marriage, or any relationship, for that matter. It is ever so much easier to punish the other person who has wronged us especially where the wrong is so egregious. I am not advocating that all mistakes can or should be forgiven. But, doesn't the act of forgiveness start with recognition that we too could have easily made the same mistake? And when we put ourselves in the shoes of another person we are taking the first step toward showing compassion to that person.

I have often wondered if my marriage to Brian would have become a love story like a few couples we knew. Would it have become a love story worth the sacrifice of parts of myself? I like to think so but our time together was cut so short—only six years, half of which Brian was sick. We were on the right track. I felt a bond with Brian that I can't describe. I don't know if we would have made it work for fifty or more years. I do know that we had much to forgive each other for.

I really didn't have much time to grieve or to dwell on my lost love for Brian or my incredible hurt over his relationship with Kendra and his silence about it. I had other pressing people in my life who desperately needed my love and compassion—my children. There are no words to describe the total emotional and physical exhaustion I experienced right before Brian died. I hoped my well of compassion had not run dry.

One of my goals throughout the trauma of Brian's illness was to have no regrets. I promised him we would care for him at home until the end. I was able to do that with a lot of help. I wanted to take care of and treat Brian they way I would want to be treated if I was in his shoes, so to speak. Of course I had times when I was definitely not kind, loving, or patient. In fact, I was quite the opposite. Sometimes I was angry that he just wouldn't die and get this over with. I often blamed him for taking so long to die, as if he had any control over it. I can remember a time when I could hardly be in the same room with him because I felt like I was suffocating. Other times I just didn't want to let him go. For a while I beat myself up, mercilessly, over those failings. I finally accepted that I had done the best I could. I could have done much better but I can't change that now. I think Brian knew that I loved him and that I did the best I could for him. Maybe I am learning to be kind to myself and to forgive myself for not being perfect or always doing the right thing. When I am kind to myself and recognize that I do not always have to meet some exacting standard of behavior, and when I can forgive myself for not meeting those unrealistic standards, I am practicing self-compassion.

In my quest to give Brian the best that I could and to make his time as comfortable as possible, I inadvertently thwarted my other goal of sparing the children as much pain and suffering as possible. I put Brian's needs above everyone else's including the children. I shielded the children from the physical demands of caring for a terminally ill father. I made a point of not asking them for much help in that area. What I failed to see was that Brian's presence in the house made it impossible to shield the older children from the brutal reality of watching someone you love die a horrible, agonizing death. It wasn't a real problem where Gary was concerned because he was so young. With Gary, I tried to maintain a normal routine for him, to shield him as much as possible from the stress and anger, and to surround him with love. He wouldn't be aware of the pain until he was much older.

If I had realized the scope of the damage to the children, I may have made other choices. I kept my promise to Brian but at what a price to my children? The first-hand witnesses to this nightmare, the children, may have suffered the most. I was focused on doing what was best for the dying. Should I have been focused on doing what was best for the living? As I evaluate my choices, in retrospect I think that sending Brian to a nursing home might have sent the wrong message to the children regarding how we care for terminally ill loved ones. But I didn't think about that at the time.

I have struggled with whether I did the right thing by my children for many, many years. Occasionally when I see a terminally ill person or someone in a wheelchair, I will beat myself up over my treatment of Brian. When I find myself starting down that path of inconsolable recrimination, I stop and remind myself that I really did the best I could. I gave all that I had and then some. Can we ask anything else of ourselves? I am still learning to practice self-compassion, and so I must remind myself that what I did was all that I could do—and what else can anyone ask of themselves?

I have no idea who made the arrangements to have Brian's body removed from the house. There was a police officer at the house when I arrived home, so I guess he did. It didn't happen immediately, and I was thankful for that. I never entered the room again while Brian's body was in there. But I wanted the children to have the opportunity to say goodbye to Brian if they wanted to. "Kind of silly," I remember thinking, "because there is nothing in there but a lifeless, cold body."

"There is an emergency at home. I need Jessica to come home right away," I said to the manager of the store where my eldest daughter had a part time job. I didn't ask to speak to Jessica directly because I knew she would hear something in my voice. As I waited for Jessica to arrive home, I called a few people including my friend Norma. I didn't want to be alone with my thoughts. Keeping busy has always served me well as a coping mechanism as long as I am careful not to let it take over. Norma was much older than I, and she had already lost her husband. I knew she would understand.

"Brian died today," I told Norma. I heard a scream behind me. I turned around to see Jessica standing there white as a ghost.

"I didn't get to say goodbye!" she shrieked. I caught her just as she started to collapse. We sat on the couch and talked. I don't remember what we said. I felt like I was outside my body watching these events. Someone else was talking to Jessica and doing these things, not me. Jessica elected to say goodbye to Brian. I walked her to the door of the room. I thought she might change her mind. After she went into the room, I turned and walked away.

I then started calling the home of the friends of my other two children to locate them. They had a habit of not being where they said they were. Somehow I must have located them because I know that each of the three older children entered the room and stayed for a period of time before Brian's body was taken away. We have never discussed what transpired in the room during those visits. I only know that I heard that same shrieking sound that I had made and that each child emerged pale and exhausted. The sound of that shriek can still paralyze me. I know because I occasionally hear it during TV broadcasts regarding the war. It is the sound death makes in the living. To say that it sends shivers up my spine would be an understatement, but I can't find any other words to describe its effect on me.

I never saw the children weep much after that day. They would grieve in other less healthy ways. The funeral and viewing were not as difficult as I thought they would be. I think I was just numb, and I was busy. There were people all around for that first week. I almost broke down when one of Brian's oldest friends come to the funeral home. He said hello to me, walked into a pew, sat down in that pew, quietly bowed his head, and then sobbed uncontrollably. He seemed unaware that anyone else was present. Even now I can still see him crying uncontrollably.

"Should I have Gary view Brian's body?" I asked my psychologist friend.

"Wow, I will have to think about that and get back to you," he responded. His answer was he didn't know. Gary was about two and half at the time. The family was having a private viewing just before the general viewing. When we arrived, the casket was already at the front of the memorial chapel. The casket was open at Brian's request. He wore the suit that just a short time earlier he had purchased for a very special occasion. He had never spent that much money on a suit before. He looked very handsome then and now. The four older children were sitting a few rows back from where the casket was located. I picked Gary up in my arms and carried him up to the casket.

What do you say to a two-and-a-half-year-old in such a situation? Brian had been sick for Gary's entire life. Gary had accepted the man sitting in the corner of the room in the lifeless body as a normal part of his life. Often when he was sitting in that chair, Brian would ask for a drink of water. There was always a cup with a straw in it sitting on the table next to Brian. I would put the straw up to his mouth so he could take a drink. I would sometimes hear Brian making some fearful sounds, and when I looked up, I would see Gary putting the straw up to Brian's mouth. Brian's eyes were literally popping out of his head in terror. Gary kept trying to put the straw in Brian's mouth. I didn't want to yell at

Gary, so I would quickly cross the room and gently take the cup from Gary saying, "Daddy is not thirsty now, but thank you."

Now, in the lobby of the funeral home, I tritely said, "Daddy has gone to heaven." Gary and I stayed only a moment at the casket. Gary looked at Brian and was silent. I didn't have Gary touch the body because the sensation of the cold flesh is so frightening. I carried Gary to the lobby in my arms.

"My daddy died," Gary calmly said to my father. My father and I gasped and choked back tears.

"I know," said my father. My father took Gary in his arms, hugged him, and took him home.

Gary seemed to accept death as a part of life. He never asked any questions about it. He never cried. He never seemed frightened by it. Maybe he was wise enough to realize that it was merely the lifeless body in which his father was trapped that had finally given out. If only we adults could be as accepting of and unafraid of death as children. Throughout this ordeal, Gary was my comfort and a source of my strength. His hugs, kisses, and statements of "I love you" were like salve on an open wound. All of this emanated from a child that almost didn't come into this world because I was afraid. Thankfully the cancer appeared in my uterus when it did. If it had waited a few more months to manifest itself, Gary would not have been conceived because by then Brian was already sick.

The next day we held a memorial service at our church. It was beautiful, or so I was told. I didn't hear any of it. I remember walking in with the children and seeing the church overflowing. I don't remember anything else about the service except for the soloist singing "Amazing Grace." "Taps" was played at the graveside ceremony. I hadn't expected that. It stirred something in all of us because we gathered around and clung to each other with tears in our eyes. I still can't hear "Taps" or "Amazing Grace" without shedding tears, sometimes uncontrollably.

When the funeral was over the attendees all disappeared back into their daily lives. The older children returned to school or at least they said they did. Many, many days I don't think I would have even gotten out of bed if it weren't for Gary. He needed to be taken care of. He needed a mother to love him. That is not to say that the older children didn't.

As I look back on it, I realize in my grief I deserted my older children. I abandoned them. They had already been adrift without any parental supervision for some two years by the time Brian died. They lost both parents for a very long period of time. I made the wrong decisions where they were concerned. I know that now.

There was an indescribable emptiness in my life after Brian died. Some days it almost seemed as if I had imagined him. One day my life was all about caring for him and the next day he was gone. In spite of knowing that this would happen it was a shock. The people who I did interact with right after Brian's death avoided talking to me about Brian and our life together. I guess they were afraid it would upset me. That reinforced the eerie feeling that he was never here and that none of it was real. I was reminded of how I used to feel when I watched that TV show *The Twilight Zone*. What was real? The song from that show can still make me feel disconnected from reality and fearful. I wanted to remember Brian and the life we shared—not forget it.

Ten years of my life seemed to vanish along with Brian. When I looked back, I saw only a huge void. In the beginning when I felt choked by loss, fear, and emptiness I could run to the phone and call his sister, Nancy. Talking to Nancy took the edge off the pain. It had happened. Brian had been here. We had shared some wonderful years together. I wasn't losing my mind. Now Nancy is gone.

A therapist friend, along with Nancy, understood the overpowering need I had to talk about Brian and our life together. He and his wife would come visit and we could share stories about Brian and remember the good times and things about our life and about Brian before he got sick. I would feel almost joyful during their visits. It so helped to ease the pain of the loss. Sadly, they moved away for a job opportunity elsewhere.

These were brief moments in a very dark time. These were moments when people who also cared for Brian could share their love of him with me. I understood that not everyone loved Brian the way Nancy or I did. But do we have to share the love of the lost one to share in the person's grief? I think that is what compassion is all about. We call upon the feelings of loss or pain we have experienced in our own loves to reach out to others who are experiencing loss and pain. We don't have to have known the deceased to feel that person's pain. And just reaching out to the other person helps them weather their own grief. Someone understands. Someone cares. "I am not alone" is the message they receive when we show them compassion. But it cannot be empty words. Saying the obligatory "I am sorry for your loss" doesn't ease any pain and in fact can often seem a slight because it is uncaring. I do so wish more of us were not afraid to tap into our own feelings because it is there compassion is born and compassion heals. Sadly, I did not find much of that at this time in my life, and I think that is why it was such an incredibly dark time.

We anchor a cold hard stone in the ground with a name, date of birth, and date of death. Why do we do that? I could imagine Brian was just at work or away on a business trip until I saw that stone. I would run my fingers over the etching and say the name out loud. It was so permanent. It was so final. Somehow I would be prone on the fresh dirt with my forehead pressed into the cold hard stone. My body was convulsing and tears were flooding my checks. I know because the stone was wet. At night the cemetery was a solitary place. I could sob, punch the dirt, and scream. Why Brian? Why do I have to go through this? Why do I have to raise my children alone again? This is so unfair! Why did this happen to me? I hate God! I am so alone! I can't do this. I found myself there many nights. For a while every outing to attend anything ended at the cemetery. I now understood that a cemetery is a place for the living. It is a place where they can grieve.

I didn't live in the present much that first year after Brian died. My thoughts and my feelings were directed to and focused in the past. I lived, over and over in my mind, the events of my life with Brian. There was no chronology to it. It was a mass of jumbled images and events from our life together. As hard as I tried I couldn't bring myself back to the present. None of the memories were of any significant event. It was the simple mundane stuff of life. It played over and over again in my head like one of those old-time reel home movies. It went in reverse. It went forward. It flickered. It fluttered. It came apart. It kept going. I had no control over it. It controlled me. I was helpless to guide it or stop it.

Since that time I can't remember all the details as vividly as I did that first year. They have continued to fade. Maybe life is not so unkind.

No one called. No one came to visit. When the phone did ring I would run to answer it. I always, unconsciously, expected to hear it. "Hi, honey, how are you?" Brian would always say when I answered the phone in the way only he could say it. Of course it was never him on the other end of the phone. If there is an emptier feeling that what I experienced when I answered that phone, I don't know it or want to know it.

Where did everyone go? In truth they had all pretty much vanished during the course of Brian's illness. They all came to his funeral though. Maybe the better question to ask is why did all of our friends disappear when Brian was ill? Perhaps in Brian's case it was too difficult to watch someone die such a horrible death especially when you can't really help them in any medical or physical way. Perhaps seeing Brian reminded everyone of their own mortality and it frightened them to think this or something as horrible could happen to them too. Perhaps it brings up memories of other deaths they have never fully processed and don't want to open that wound again, i.e., that old out of sight, out of mind way of dealing with some of life's challenges. Maybe people only liked Brian when he could do things for them. I expect it was different reasons for different people depending on their relationship with Brian when he was healthy.

If people only knew the power of a simple visit and how much emotional pain was alleviated by that simple act of caring, maybe they would have made the effort to see Brian. A visit to Brian was certainly painful as the visitor witnessed immeasurable physical and emotional suffering. We prefer to run away from suffering, and pain. We are frightened if an event will call those things up in us. But heartache teaches us so much and a simple act of compassion generates incredibly wonderful feelings of love, healing and more in both the giver and receiver. A simple act of caring would have helped Brian, the children and I so much.

I remember taking Gary to a parade we used to go to with Brian every year. Samuel had marched in the parade years earlier. Gary and I were sitting on bleachers. There was a married couple sitting in front of us. I leaned forward. I couldn't stop myself. I tried. I embarrassed myself. I was an intruder. I leaned in so close my face almost touched the wife's hair. All I wanted was to listen to the conversation. Oh, I wasn't interested in what they were saying. That was of no interest to me. I was interested in how they were saying it. You see, they were speaking that intimate talk married couples use. You know, part words, part silence, part looks, and part body language or gestures spoken in a certain low, familiar tone of voice. I remember thinking how I wished I had skipped the parade that day.

The list of losses went on and on and on. It seemed infinite. I was compelled by some unknown force to remember as many events of the past ten years as possible in that one year. With Brian's death the entire last ten years of my life was wiped out. It felt like they were gone. When they buried Brian, they buried our life together—my part included. We were both buried that day. At least the biggest part of me was buried that day. I was left to rebuild a life with the remnants. They seemed pretty paltry at the time. I am reminded of that line in Tristan and Isolde. I thought it was so stupid at the time—romantic nonsense. What was it? It went something like, "They drank death together."

I felt buried just like Brian—buried, or better yet, maybe crushed beneath the weight of pain, loss, and suffering. The world, the people in it and their problems and concerns all seemed so trivial, and meaningless. People would talk to me and it was as if we were separated by a wall —a wall of grief and pain. I felt totally isolated from the world by my experience.

There were days when I could hardly get out of bed and nights when I didn't sleep at all. Some days I felt like I glowed red with anger at God, the world, life, and everyone who had not lost a loved one. Those were dark days.

It is almost as if the world believed everything was fine now that Brian's suffering was over. They didn't realize that the suffering of myself and my children was now taking on epic proportions. A kind friend asked me what she could do to help and I suggested she bring dinner over. So she did. However, she would appear with the dinner. Put in on the counter and announce she was late to take her child somewhere. She was in the house perhaps five or ten minutes. In the throes of grief, it is difficult to know what you want and very difficult to put anything into words. I didn't really need the food. I wanted someone to come to the house and spend a short time with me. I realize that now. I was hurt when she would drop off the food and race out the door, but I never said anything. I was afraid she would not come back. Going through the motions and checking off on your to-do list an obligatory visit sick friend or visit grieving friend really doesn't help.

I was trying to rejoin the world. I was driving to an acquaintance's house one evening. She lived in one of those incredibly annoying developments where all the streets have these cutesy names, and they all run in circles. I was totally lost. This was before GPS. This was the type of place where they think too many street lights detract from the ambience of the neighborhood. It was so dark I decided to stop the car and get out to read the street sign. Fortunately, there was a lone street light at the corner ahead. I pulled the car over to the curb and parked in the opposite direction of the flow of traffic. I opened my car door. As I looked down to make sure I wasn't stepping into a drainage ditch, I saw it. It was stamped into the concrete on that sidewalk. In fact, it was stamped into the concrete all over that city. It was the logo for Brian's construction company. It was a logo he had designed. I can remember when he first showed me that logo. He was so proud of it.

"Can I help you, miss?" the man asked. I must have looked ridiculous dressed in a suit and heels at a construction site. Mud and dirt were everywhere.

"I am supposed to meet Brian, the president of the company, here," I replied.

The man looked at me like I was crazy. "He doesn't come to the job sites, miss." Just then a white Lincoln Town Car rounded the corner. Brian was at the wheel. The man shook his head incredulously and returned to his crew. That day I got my first lesson in building a sidewalk.

You see, Brian and I were on opposite sides of a lawsuit and Brian had agreed to explain one of the construction issues to me. We walked around the site together while he explained how to build a sidewalk. Brian was so proud when he showed me his company logo stamped in the concrete sidewalk. I can see him, smell him and feel his presence even as I write this. It is the small memories that ignite the flame of grief. Funny, I thought it would be the big days, the important days like Christmas and other holidays that would be the most difficult to get through. It turns out you can prepare yourself for the big days. The little memories just kind of sneak up on you. Seeing that logo stamped into the sidewalk propelled me back to that day. I started to cry. I turned my car around and headed home. I never made it to her house.

CHAPTER TEN

Living in a World of Grief

THERE SEEMED TO BE NO END TO MY CHILDREN'S SUFFERING AND THE trouble they got themselves into as they acted out their pain and grief. I had to stand by and watch as their anger and grief spun destructively out of control.

Eventually I realized that I couldn't help them because they didn't want my help, and that was a deep pain of another kind. I felt an overwhelming sense of failure and abject helplessness. I honestly didn't think they would ever come back from all of this. I was sure Samuel and Ellen would end up in prison or dead.

Those were the darkest of days for all of us but we did get through them and we even flourished. We learned compassion for the people in our lives who either totally avoided us or simply engaged in behaviors familiar to them like judgment, blame and condemnation. In the end, we were able to forgive the world and God. We grew ever so much closer to each other as a result of this gut wrenching experience because we were able to be compassionate with each other. But it was a long and painful journey.

"Is this Samuel's mother?" the voice on the other end of the phone ominously asked.

"Yes," I replied. "We need you to come down to the police station to pick up your son," the police officer said. It was drugs. The police stopped Samuel and some friends while they were driving in Samuel's car. They found marijuana in a backpack in the car. It was a stroke of luck that the young man Samuel hardly knew told the police it was his marijuana. They were minors. Samuel was released into my custody. He would not face any charges. The officer could not have been any nicer.

"He is a good kid with a future. He is not like the other kid who had the drugs. Take him home and keep him out of trouble," the officer said to me. I hoped he was right. I hoped I could do that.

I received a similar call or should I say many similar calls regarding Ellen. "Your daughter was driving around in a car with some friends. She has violated curfew," the voice on the other end of the phone said.

"Can you keep her in jail for the night?" I asked.

"No, ma'am. She is a minor. You have to come pick her up." Jessica was home, so I left Gary and went to pick Ellen up at the police station. It was approximately three a.m. I don't know what Ellen's official punishment was but mine was to sit through an eight-hour class on a Saturday with other "bad" parents and discuss our kids' behavior. I guess I deserved that and maybe more.

Samuel and Ellen's presence at school was something of a nightmare for them and I guess for the teachers as well. I was called to the school on a regular basis for conferences about my children. "Please sit here," the school principal said as he pointed to the chair at the head of the long conference table. The hostility in the room was palpable. Six pairs of eyes had been glaring at me since I entered the room. "I called this meeting to discuss Ellen's behavior," the principal announced. "We are all aware that Ellen's stepfather had a terminal illness and has died," he said. Those were the only kind words spoken during this thirty-minute meeting. You see, Ellen, was "stupid, incorrigible, disruptive to the class, and would never amount to anything." Oh, the teachers who were present at that meeting didn't say that to me that day—at least not in those words. They reserved those exact words for Ellen when she was in class. I didn't know that until later. You see, she was just a bad kid, and I was just a bad mother. The school and teachers were sending that message loud and clear. This was just the first of such meetings.

Is it any surprise that Ellen eventually simply stopped attending school? Oh, I am not saying that is the only reason for her lack of attendance. There were a lot of other contributing factors, but I would have to say the attitude of the teachers and administration probably topped the list. Who would want to go to a place every day where you are told what a bad person you are? How different would Ellen's life be now and then if instead of berating her they had put their arm around her shoulder and asked her if they could do anything for her? Such a simple gesture would surely take less energy than the berating did. They never did. The teachers and administrators never showed any compassion for either Ellen or Samuel during the entire three years of Brian's illness or after he died. There was never a kind or compassionate word spoken. They were just annoyed that my children were a problem. They simply wanted them gone from the school.

How do I know some compassion from the teachers or administrators would have made a difference in their lives? Because there was one teacher who did that for Ellen. It was no surprise that Ellen not only wasn't a troublemaker but actually did well in her class. That fact seemed to be lost on her other teachers.

I have often wondered why the teachers' knowledge of the terrible situation at home didn't translate into any compassion for my children. Certainly compassion requires time for reflection. The feelings that give rise to compassion have to be nurtured and tended to. When we are busy all the time, we simply move from one task to another without giving much thought to our own feelings much less the feelings and situations of others we come into contact with. But it was more than busyness that was preventing the teachers or administrators from showing compassion to my children. They couldn't see that my children's behavior was an acting out of their incredible pain and grief.

The teachers spent their time and energy judging and condemning me and my children. I'm sure they thought we were all handling the situation rather poorly, and if we were tougher or better we wouldn't be having these issues or problems. My children weren't strong enough. I wasn't a good parent because I couldn't control my children. Those were some of the spoken and unspoken messages I received at the conferences and during other interactions with the school personnel. It reminded me so much of the earlier time in our lives when I had experienced something similar as a divorced, single mother. Only I think this time I was even more shocked by the lack of compassion because no one could blame me for my circumstances as they had when I was divorced. Certainly people would show compassion in the face of a terminal illness, but they didn't.

You see, I don't think any of them ever put themselves in our shoes. They never tried to imagine what it must be like to lose your father or husband in such a horrible way or what it must be like to be a witness on a daily basis to incredible suffering and pain. That pain shaped our family's daily psyche and interactions for more than three years by the time Brian died. Perhaps they had never experienced any kind of loss that would allow them to relate to us, but I doubt that. Somewhere in their lives they had experienced some pain that could have been a catalyst for compassion.

An act of compassion can be a simple thing. Showing they cared about the suffering of Samuel and Ellen could have eased their pain and suffering tremendously. They could have offered some kind words, something like, "I know you are going through a very difficult time. Is there anything I can do to help you?" They could have asked any of us what it was like. They could have tried to imagine our lives. My children were acting out their pain, but no one seemed to recognize that.

I would have settled for the teachers just refraining from sending messages to them that they were bad people. That is not to say that my children's bad behavior should have been acceptable. I just think there were much better ways of dealing with their behavior.

"No, I will not be attending any more parent teacher conferences," I said to the assistant principal.

"I quite frankly don't understand your attitude," he responded.

"I really can't handle any more kid-bashing sessions at this time in my life," I said as I hung up the phone. That was the last time I ever spoke to him.

After Brian died, I took the two middle children to Dr. Thompson, a psychologist, on a weekly basis. He was a very wise man. "They will grieve when they are ready and in their own way." He was so right.

I sat with Samuel and Ellen in the evenings and tried to do their homework with them. I attended parent nights and spoke to individual teachers. I drove them to school myself every day. I ordered them to come home right after school. I kept them in after school activities they enjoyed. I tried to stay in touch with their friend's parents. In short, I tried to everything I could think of. But ultimately they needed me much earlier when Brian was sick, and I wasn't there. It was too late for me to help them by this point but I wouldn't realize that until after we had all suffered so much more.

"Ellen, we need to talk about what is going on with you," I said. I turned away for a moment, and when I looked back Ellen had run out of the room and was headed up the stairs to her bedroom.

"Stop right now!" I screamed at Ellen as I chased her up the stairs. I caught her and grabbed her by the arm.

Ellen whirled around to look at me. She had such a look of hatred, loathing and rage I was taken aback. "You are a stupid b****!" she screamed at me. I slapped her in the face. She went up to her bedroom and locked the door. It was hard finding the energy to battle with these teenagers. I realize now that they probably thought I didn't care. They were probably right some of the time. I so wanted a respite from problems for a while.

A few days later the doorbell rang. A man in a suit was standing at my door. "I am from Child Protective Services. Your daughter Ellen came to school with a small bruise on her face." She would pick that day to go to school! "She said you slapped her. I need to come in and look around," he said. Did I have a choice? He poked around the house for a while. Gary was asleep, but he examined him very closely for bruises. Fortunately for me, prior to coming to the house, he had spoken to the social worker who had assisted us during Brian's illness. Thankfully, because of her intervention, the inquiry ended there but not before he went to see my eldest daughter, Jessica, at high school. She was humiliated to say the least. Only she could give Ellen a tongue lashing that Ellen would heed. Would we ever be able forgive each other for all the terrible things we had done and said to each other?

When I returned from work or some errands there were all kinds of unsavory people in the house—Ellen's "friends." Some of my jewelry went missing. After I confronted Ellen about her friends and the missing jewelry a few times, she simply stopped bringing friends home and she stopped spending any time at home. Samuel was always stoned.

"Ellen, Ellen, wake up. It is time for school," I said as I shook her. I tried to wake her up for ten minutes or more. She would try to open her eyes, but then she would fall back to sleep. I couldn't understand why I couldn't wake her up. I turned and left the room. I thought Ellen was sick or depressed. In reality, Ellen was out all night doing drugs and sleeping all day. I never even considered that as an option. I thought she hung around with a bad crowd and was not attending school regularly, but I didn't see what was really going on. I had never done drugs, so I didn't know the signs or symptoms. Maybe there was just too much going on for me to focus on what her behavior really meant. I am sure I wouldn't have known how to cope with her behavior even if I had known. I found out much later that she apparently drove one of the cars at night after I went to sleep. She was only fourteen.

"This is Sue in the attendance office," the voice on the other end of the phone said. "Samuel is not at school today."

"Okay," I said and hung up the phone. The phone rang again a few minutes later.

"This is Sue in the attendance office" she said. "Ellen is not at school today."

Those phone calls became part of my morning ritual along with my cup of coffee. I have no idea what Samuel and Ellen did after I dropped them off at school. I asked, but they didn't answer me. I knew I wouldn't get a straight answer anyway. I'm not sure I could have handled the truth then if they told me. I berated them and told them they needed to attend school but I didn't do much more.

Maybe part of my coping mechanism was to put my head in the sand when it came to my children. I didn't have the strength to really discipline them. Somehow I deluded myself into thinking that they were working through their grief. I lost control over Samuel and Ellen when Brian was sick. I was stretched well beyond my limits in caring for Brian and Gary, and I had not time or energy for anyone or anything else. But that is no excuse. After Brian died I could not get any control back over those two. They had been unsupervised for far too long.

The calls from the police and the school continued. I received several calls from the police department regarding Samuel. I picked him up several times from various police departments. His problems were drug-related as well. He never acted out like Ellen. He was much more silent in his grief and anger. I expressed my anger and disappointment to him. I really didn't know what else to do. I feel fortunate that neither of them ended up in a juvenile detention facility. Maybe things weren't as bad as they could have been after all.

By day, I was the mother of a charming preschooler attending coffees with other moms or I was working in a responsible position in the legal field. But I wasn't really part of that life. I couldn't connect to anything or anyone. I was on the outside looking in. I was an empty shell going through the motions of everyday living. I would listen while people talked to me. I would wonder how they could be so angry because their husband left his clothes on the floor or be upset over something that was said or done by someone at the office. At that time in my life their concerns and even their lives seemed silly—not funny silly, stupid silly, insipid. I know they didn't want to hear about my life. That's good because I really didn't want to talk about it. I wanted to forget about it for a while if that was possible.

I was bitter and angry that others weren't going through what I was going through when Brian was ill. I know I would have been less bitter if people had shown some compassion. I ended up cutting myself off from other people while Brian was sick. "If I talk to my friends about my husband, I won't have any friends to talk to," an acquaintance whose husband was suffering from the same illness told me. She was much wiser than I. I didn't take her advice. I simply didn't know how to talk about mundane things during that time. As I look back, I realize I could have handled my interactions with others so much better and so I also blame myself.

One of my closest friends simply stopped calling me after we received Brian's diagnosis. At the end no one ever visited him but his sister Nancy and her husband. Thank heaven for them.

"Mom, Mom," the voice was a mix of fear, desperation and anger. Someone was shaking me. I awoke to a semi-conscious state to see

Jessica standing over my bed. "Ellen has a guy in her room," Jessica said. Through force of habit I looked at the clock. Gary was asleep next to me on the bed. It was three o'clock in the morning. I got up and Jessica and I went to Ellen's room. The door was closed. I hesitated. I wanted to just turn and walk away, but I forced myself to push it open, not knowing what I would find. Ellen was standing alone in the middle of the room.

"Ellen, where is he?" I demanded. I turned, and with a huge feeling of trepidation, I pushed the door open to the closet. Ellen was not known for making good choices regarding friends these last few years. As I pushed open the door, I wondered if I was going to have to call the police. He left when I told him to. What a relief!

After I escorted Ellen's friend out of the house and locked the door, I put on the alarm. I never thought I would have to use the alarm to keep my kids in and their friends out. For a long time, I thought I was the only one with the code, but apparently I wasn't. Samuel and Ellen apparently knew it. It didn't matter. Knowing Ellen, if she didn't have the code, she would have just left and let the alarm screech. As I turned to go back to bed, Jessica gave me a tongue lashing. I deserved it.

"That was her drug dealer," she told me. My first thought was it could have been worse. I knew Jessica was disappointed in me. I also knew it was not Jessica's job to police Ellen. I just couldn't seem to find the wherewithal to do anything about these things. I went into my bedroom and closed the door. If only it were that easy to shut the world out. But wasn't I already doing that?

We had no support from anyone during that time in our lives. My parents had come back into our lives before Brian and I married but they never called me during that time. They rarely came to visit. In fact, I begged them to come visit for Christmas during what would be Brian's last Christmas. They said they were going to spend Christmas with my sister instead. I wouldn't have time to process all of this until much later.

Ellen and Samuel's behavior ostracized us even more. Even before their behavior had totally deteriorated the parents of their friends or other school mates did not want my children to be at their house or to be with their children.

Sometimes I wonder if some of those people had just reached out to my children and permitted them to come over to a house that was not all about pain, suffering, and death, it could have stemmed the tide of the behaviors. No one threw them a lifeline. They continued their downward slide. Compassion was totally missing from their lives. At a bare minimum it would have helped if others simply stopped treating them like they were terrible people and saw them instead as children in tremendous emotional pain.

I took the children to church with us for a while when Brian was sick. Brian would attend church in the wheelchair. They would attend Sunday school. Often the Sunday school teacher would come to see me after church and complain about Samuel and Ellen's behavior. He asked me, not in so many words, not to bring them anymore because they disrupted the class. Was it any wonder they stopped going to church also? How different would their lives have been then and now if that teacher had shown them some compassion? They were in unrelenting pain and no one seemed to understand or care. They still bear the scars.

This sounds rather matter-of-fact, but in reality, it was far from that. Ellen was in a rage that lasted for years. She screamed at me, used every conceivable expletive, called me every conceivable name, and did whatever she pleased. I get exhausted just thinking about this. I don't have the emotional energy to relate the entire litany of behaviors, arguments, or vicious scenes because to do so, I would have to relive it at least in my mind. I simply can't do that again. Once was more than enough to live through that time with Ellen. I am not sure I even can remember it all as thankfully my memories of this have faded. I am unaware of much of what she did do as a lot of it took place away from the house. She was rarely home. When she was she reminded me of the Tasmanian devil, the cartoon character. He races through the desert spreading a lot of dust. Ellen whirled through the house, school, and I imagine everyplace else spreading rage and fear wherever she went. I can still feel her anger and my fear as I write this.

"It is very difficult to turn a minor over to the care of the state, but it can be done," the social worker said. She was the same social worker who had helped us through the final months of Brian's illness. I felt comfortable talking to her. I was absolutely desperate. I can't begin to describe my level of desperation. I had to be or I never would have considered such an option.

"What happens to her if I do that?" I asked the social worker. I can't remember exactly what she said. All I remember is that it didn't sound very appealing. In addition, I didn't have the energy for another battle even if the outcome would be good, and it appeared this outcome was not what I was looking for. Ellen needed to be under someone or something's control for her own good and mine, but where was I to find that? I think it was just a fantasy I explored for a time. Just thinking I actually had an option gave me the illusion that I had some control, and that made things more bearable on those particularly hard days dealing with Ellen.

I think I was patient and loving at least some of the time. Maybe I wasn't. I know I tried to calmly talk to Samuel and Ellen about how they felt and what they were going through. The minute I asked a question about how she was feeling, Ellen's eyes would flash with anger and she would say something very cruel to me. Maybe she thought it should be obvious to me how she felt. She was so angry and I was unable to respond with love rather than anger. Usually we ended up in a heated argument. Perhaps I was the one acting like an adolescent. Her emotions were so raw, so exposed, that just a simple question could ignite a fire of emotion expressed only as anger. Why was anger the only emotion we permitted ourselves to express? If only I had reached out and tried to hug her. I guess we were all torn down to our roots and maybe beyond. We wouldn't be able to connect until we had rebuilt some of our own foundations.

I tried to set up some structure for them and to discipline them after Brian died. I couldn't lock them up in the house. I couldn't be with them every minute of the day. I think I still cared about them, but sometimes I wasn't sure. Most of the time I just wanted them to go away and leave me alone. I felt suffocated by their problems. I felt guilty because I believed if I had handled things better they wouldn't be having these problems. I had absolutely no idea what to do. If I sent them away, I was afraid they would think I didn't love them or they would feel totally alone and rejected—more than I imagined they already did. Maybe I didn't love them anymore. Is it possible to stop loving your child? I didn't know the answer at that time. I know I didn't feel any love toward them.

Eventually I just ran out of energy to fight them and to fight for them. It was sadly a constant battle and a losing one at that. Samuel was not as overtly hostile and confrontational as Ellen. He simply, for the most part, ignored me. It was me against Ellen and Samuel, or me against their friends, or me against the school. And it was them against the world. It was a war. Everyone was losing. The calls continued to come. The situation and the children's behavior continued to deteriorate.

"This is Krishna, Samuel's employer. Samuel has stolen a scale from the store."

"A what?" I asked.

"A scale we use to measure the meats for the sandwiches," his employer said.

"That sounds totally ridiculous. What would Samuel want with a scale for measuring lunch meat?" I asked.

"They use it to weigh drugs," she replied. "I am going to report him to the police unless you pay for it," she said.

I had pushed him into getting this job so he could spend his time constructively. I talked to Samuel. He denied it. My sense was that he was telling the truth. She really had no proof that Samuel had taken it. There were a lot of other young people working there. "I won't pay for it," I called his employer to tell her.

"I will call the police," she said.

"Okay," I said and I hung up the phone. Within a few minutes I was hunched over the toilet vomiting. I called her back. "How much do you want? I will send you a check," I said.

"When can Samuel come back to work?" she asked. I hung up the phone.

We all grieve in our own way. For adolescents, not surprisingly, they act out their grief, or at least two of mine did. I didn't understand that at the time. I thought if they were truly grieving we would be huddling together, talking, and crying. Why do I continue to insist on imposing unrealistic expectations on situations and others? They only create havoc, pain, and disappointment. When will I learn that? How or why would I expect my children's behavior to meet my idealized expectations? How much easier life would be if emotions fit into designated categories and were expressed by designated behaviors? Grief from death = crying and tears. As I write this, I can't imagine how I could expect that to be so. There is a wrong and right way to grieve, isn't there? How arrogant of me to think so.

Sometimes I looked at the children's behavior as a slap in the face. I acted as if it was personally directed at me. They were making my life difficult when I wanted to curl up in a cocoon and heal. I was resentful and angry at them. They forced me back into the world of problems way too soon. As one friend succinctly put it, "You can't put an adult head on a child." Still I resented them for it. If I only I could have put my own feelings aside to see that, through their actions, they were really crying out in pain. I thought I had learned that lesson in my marriage counseling with Brian but I guess some lessons take a long time to learn or at least put into practice. How different would this difficult time have been for all of us if I had done that? I know my response exacerbated and even ignited the situation.

I never stopped loving Ellen. She was my daughter. But I could not imagine that I would ever like Ellen again or that I would ever want to spend time with her again. Ellen's anger consumed her and me and everything in her path. She was in a constant state of rage. Samuel was just a lost soul.

"Why don't you send them away?" he asked. "I have a client whose son became disrespectful and she immediately packed him off to military school. She said it was the best thing she had ever done," continued my friend.

"We have children so they can be a part of our lives. We don't send them away the minute things get difficult. I don't want to send them a message that I am abandoning or giving up on them. I need to do everything I can before I take that drastic step," I replied.

Eventually I ran out of ideas. Everything I tried had failed. I realized that I had absolutely no idea how to help them or what to do for them. I sent them both to those survival camps for a summer. They flourished there, but when they returned home, they reverted to their old behaviors and friends. I don't know why I didn't expect that would happen. I must have called a dozen boarding schools looking for one that would take my two children. Still I didn't want to send them away. I thought I should be able to help them. After all, I was their mother. I hoped they would eventually work through their issues. As more time passed, I realized that wasn't going to happen, at least not before someone was seriously injured or serious damage was done. Maybe I didn't do it out of selfishness. I think I was afraid of being even lonelier if they went away. I think the crises with them prevented me from dealing with my own emotions. After all, I was a crisis junkie. Maybe I was just afraid to admit failure. I talked about it and I thought about it, but I couldn't find the wherewithal to send them away.

Finally, my relationship with Warren gave me the strength to do what was best for my children. I had to recognize and accept that I couldn't help them and that they would be better off somewhere else away from the bad environment. This was more than two years after Brian had died. Warren encouraged and cajoled me into making the decision. I am grateful to Warren for that, even though I later realized that he did not do that out of an altruistic desire to help the children or me. It is a paradox that some of the best things in life have their inception in impure motives. So it was with the decision to send Ellen and Samuel away to military school. How fortunate we all were that Brian's life insurance provided us with some financial options I know are not available to many people.

"We can do that. Yes. We would use off-duty police officers to escort them to the school," the owner of the business told me. I was sending Ellen and Samuel away to a military boarding school. I knew I couldn't get them there by myself. They would simply refuse to go like they refused to do everything else I asked them to do. "Are they violent?" he asked me.

"I don't know what they are capable of," I responded.

"We would have to bring two officers," he replied.

I honestly don't know if, at that time, I cared what happened to them. I just wanted some peace. I was losing my ability to cope. I still had Gary who needed a functioning mother. So I paid the company to provide two off-duty police officers to escort Ellen, and later Samuel, to the military boarding school. It was located many states away in the middle of a cornfield in a small town in the Midwest. I hoped they could keep them safe there. I definitely wasn't able to do it.

I often wonder what families who don't have those financial resources do. Some of those families are imprisoned by the rage and violent behavior of their children. I know because that is what happened to one of the employees at the hair salon I used to go to. I can still see the desperation in her eyes as they peered out from her haggard face. For the most part, she looked at the floor when she related her story as if she was acutely embarrassed by it all. I understood that feeling of failure and embarrassment that accompanies the feeling that you are a terrible parent. Her husband was convicted of child abuse when he tried to physically restrain their daughter by grabbing her arm to prevent her from leaving the house. Thereafter, their daughter had all the control as she indulged her craving for drugs and the unsavory lifestyle that accompanies that addiction. She victimized her parents. I don't know the outcome. I never spoke to her again. I suspect that she was resentful that I had other options. I hope things somehow worked out for her family. I hope I offered her some understanding and compassion. I certainly understood not to judge her family. Things just happen. We may never know why and does it really matter why. It only matters that it is happening. This person is in pain and we need to offer them understanding and compassion—not judgment and recrimination.

"We will be there about six o'clock in the morning. We want to take advantage of the element of surprise. We will wake her up, get her dressed and in the car before she is aware of what is happening. Please have some clothes laid out for her," the off-duty police officer told me. The night before they were scheduled to arrive, I couldn't sleep. I really hadn't slept well since I made the decision. I kept wondering if I was doing the right thing. There was a knock at the door. I opened it and pointed to Ellen's bedroom door. I went and hid in the TV room. I was afraid if I saw them take her I would lose my courage. I was shaking and crying. I poked my head out for a moment to see Ellen, looking bewildered, in between two large men being escorted out the front door of the house. I went into the bathroom and threw up. The off-duty police officer called me, later that day, to inform me that Ellen had been safely delivered to the school.

"Hi, Mom, how are you?" I froze. It was Ellen's voice. She chatted on for a few minutes describing her physical surroundings. She never mentioned that she, just yesterday, was escorted to an isolated boarding school. "I'll call you in a few days," she said and hung up the phone. I don't remember saying much. Being silent was always much safer with Ellen. I didn't hear from Samuel for several weeks, but I did speak, on a regular basis, to the administrators at the school. Samuel and Ellen were being looked after, and they were as safe as they could be. There was an added bonus that they didn't even seem angry about being there. I think they were relieved and happy to be away. "I should have done this sooner," I thought. The grieving and healing process could now really begin for me and hopefully for my children also.

I had no good tools for coping with my own pain over the loss of Brian, much less the children's pain. Where would I have learned how to deal with all of this? Doctors will talk about the physical illness in great detail, but they are not equipped to discuss the emotional impact. I guess that really is not their role in our society. In my experience, most therapists are unprepared to discuss these issues. Maybe you need to have personal experience with terminal illness and death in order to be able to help someone.

I did have one person who helped me learn to cope with the grief and pain. Nancy, Brian's sister, understood the pain and loss in part because she also loved Brian very deeply. Nancy's compassion and understanding was akin to a climber being thrown a rope to pull them out of the dark abyss into which they have fallen. Nancy gave me a lifeline. Most days I just wanted to wallow in the dark tunnel of despair and grief. Unfortunately, Nancy was confined to home and absorbed more and more with her own serious health issues at the time of Brian's death.

Still I would visit Nancy at her house or talk to her on the phone after Brian died. She would talk for hours about every detail of her illnesses, and I mean every detail. Talking about illness, any illness seemed to brighten her day. She got a glint in her eye the way newlyweds do when they talk about their loved one. I am sure that she knew more than many doctors. It was way more information than I wanted to hear. But I found myself sitting there listening and nodding my head. I wonder now how and why I could do that. But then I remember. There was an unspoken connection and bond between us. It was threaded through our conversations. We both were in the throes of pain, suffering and loss over Brian's death. I really couldn't tell you one word that Nancy said about illness or disease. I realized that I didn't really listen to the words. I listened to the love and the compassion coming from Nancy and she felt, I hope, something similar coming from me. She and her husband were the only people who came to visit or offered any emotional support throughout Brian's illness and afterwards. Her own trials and tribulations had worked to open her heart to the suffering of others.

Sarah, from our church, called and invited me to the grief group meeting to be held at the church. I didn't want to go. I had tried ALS support groups. They depressed me. It was too many people discussing too many problems—a bitch session that for some reason didn't offer me any relief. There were far too many tales of the caregiver being stretched beyond their limits or even being emotionally abused by the ill person. We caregivers took it. Did we have a choice? That was partly what was so depressing. Our only choice was to abandon our sick spouse. Was that really a choice? Afterwards I left feeling more depressed than when I went. Maybe that group just needed some leadership I thought. In spite of that depressing experience, I couldn't tell Sarah no. She had reached out to me several times already when Samuel and Ellen were still at home, and I had rebuffed all of her attempts. But I could feel her compassion and that made all the difference.

It was almost time to leave for my first grief group meeting. "I don't want to go. I need to go," I said that back and forth constantly to myself since Sarah had called to ask me to come to the meeting at church. "Why do I have to go through this same struggle every time?" I said out loud to myself as the battle raged in my head. The war was a stalemate—no resolution. "Let's see. There is laundry in the washing machine. The dishwasher needs to be unloaded." I continued to converse with myself. I went over my list of to-do items in my head or maybe out loud. I started a few of the tasks, unconsciously hoping, I would be engaged in that task and miss the meeting. But after starting a few of the tasks on my list, somehow I found myself in the car driving to the meeting. I had managed to delay my departure but I did make it, albeit late, to the first meeting of the grief group. That is one hurdle behind me.

As I entered the room, Sarah gestured to a chair next to her. After I took my seat, Sarah stood up, "My name is Sarah. I lost my husband almost eight years ago now. I still miss him." Her facial expression and demeanor were that of a person in the throes of recent grief. "Is that what I have to look forward to? Am I never going to get beyond this grief?" I asked myself. I looked at the door but there was no way to gracefully exit. I continued to talk to myself, "Is there a way I can pass on introducing myself? I hate talking about myself and my experience." I was brought back from my conversation with myself by some more teary introductions. Sarah signaled to me to introduce myself, and I said to myself, "Well, I have no choice, but I am not going to cry in front of all these strangers. Take a deep breath. Talk slowly." I stood up. I said my name. The floodgates opened, and I couldn't say a word. I fell back into my chair. "She just lost her husband," I heard Sarah compassionately explain to the group.

After twenty years, I still cry as I write this. I cry for my children who suffered so much and who grew up without a father. I cry for myself. Crying is good because it reminds me that there is much pain and grief in life. I am not victim of my circumstance but a person given a tremendous opportunity to learn and grow. This experience was a gift. It transformed me. Crying reminds me to practice compassion in my daily interactions and practicing compassion has so enriched my life.

I felt much better after I attended a grief group meeting. Not everyone had lost their husband but they had all experienced some type of loss over which they were grieving. It made me wonder if compassion and understanding can only arise out of similar or shared experiences, hurts, losses. Is that why the children and I didn't find it at school or out in the world? Would the absence of such shared experiences be a death knell for compassion?

I looked up the definition of compassion in the dictionary: Sympathetic consciousness of others distress together with a desire to alleviate it. But where does the sympathy come from? Can we only desire to alleviate it because we know how painful or difficult it is? Certainly we all have some distress in our lives that we can call upon to create compassion for the distress of others if only we are willing to tap into it. I think we just avoid feeling our own pain, and thus we cannot feel the pain of others. I am reminded again that heartache, experiencing heartache (and allowing it to heal) is the catalyst to developing compassion.

At those meetings, we shared our stories and our feelings. I was able to express my terrible grief without fear of judgment or condemnation. I felt understood, accepted and that my feelings were okay. I didn't have to keep my feelings all bottled up inside me like I did in the real world. There were no judgments in that group, just understanding. We knew each other's pain and we wanted to help alleviate that pain. We didn't have any agenda other than to receive and give comfort. The connection we felt to each other was palpable. Its effects lasted even after I left the meeting. If I found myself going to a dark place, I could close my eyes and imagine being back in that room with people who cared and supported me. I found compassion in those meetings. Without it, I could not have started on the road to healing. I would have remained stuck in my grief and loss and remained bitter and angry. Compassion did not make the difficult times disappear but it allowed me to heal and to see those difficult times in a totally different way. I saw its power and learned, first hand, how important it is to show compassion to others. I finally learned that when I let compassion work its magic on me, magical things happen.

CHAPTER ELEVEN

The Healing Power of Compassion

A COMPASSIONATE PERSON IS A PATIENT PERSON. THEY EMPATHIZE and help without a setting a time frame and without an expectation of results. They have no agenda other than to support the person in any way that person needs. When we expect a certain result especially within a certain time frame we are no longer being compassionate. This is a lesson I learned from my children.

The phone again! It seemed in those days to always be the bearer of bad news. This time the headmaster at Ellen's military school was calling me. "Ellen was caught outside after curfew last night. She was drinking. This is her fourth infraction. She is incorrigible, and we can't have her here any longer. Ellen is being expelled from school," he said. I pleaded with him to give her another chance but he wouldn't budge. I had no idea what I could do with her now. Boarding school was my last hope. Ellen's expulsion ignited the old feelings. I was angry that Brian wasn't here to help me deal with this situation. I so wanted and needed him! By this time, Brian had been gone for more than two years. Oh my God! It all started again. What did I do wrong? How could I do this to my children? How did I fail them? What should I have done differently? After all, bad children are a result of bad parents. I know at times I was not a good mother. I had my own demons that I visited on my children. I tried so hard not to do that. Is there any way to undo the damage? Ellen is so full of rage. Is it something I did? Is it something I failed to do? I know she needed more affection than I had energy to give her. If I had been a better mom, my kids would have been better equipped emotionally to deal with Brian's death. If Ellen and Samuel survived this, could the damage ever be undone? Can they ever heal? But more importantly what could I do with Ellen now that she was being expelled from military school? That needed to be my focus. I couldn't change the past.

I realized the headmaster was still talking. I have no idea what he said right after he told me she was expelled. I was totally caught up in my own thoughts. The headmaster said, "We are sending Ellen home immediately. Please make the travel arrangements." Just a few months ago, she had been promoted to a leadership position and she was babysitting for one of her teachers. How could so much go so wrong so quickly I thought as I hung up the phone.

I was in a panic. I had no idea what I would do with her. She couldn't live at home. Even though more than a year and a half had passed since she was sent away, she was still so full of anger and rage it just spilled out into everything she did and said. I sat recalling, in a panic, some of the incredibly destructive behavior she had engaged in before going away to military school. Ellen would do whatever she wanted. She was disrespectful and even hostile to everyone. She refused to go to school. She did drugs. She would be out all night and sleep all day. She hung around with the most unsavory people. She would scream at me and call me names. I just didn't think I could live like that again. I think she improved a little at school but coming home always seemed to bring out the worst in her. She could hold it together for a little while at home, but then her behavior would deteriorate after just a few weeks of being around us or, should I say, me. I concluded that she just hated me, or loathed me might be a better way to describe it. I tried, but at the end of the day I had no idea how to get along with her.

"Ellen got expelled from the military school! She is hopeless. There is nothing else you can do for her," my dad said angrily. I was shocked to hear this from my father. He is so patient and loving. This was totally out of character for him. I know he was just frustrated and upset for me. But I was thinking exactly the same thing when he said it. It is an option I said to myself. I have my father's permission to write Ellen off, to give up and simply walk away from this problem child. But it was at that moment that I also realized I couldn't do that. Perhaps I had done everything before this out of a sense of duty or a sense that good parents do these things. I don't think I had done anything out of love or compassion for Ellen for a very long time. It was exactly when I had permission or the option to give up that I realized I didn't want to. I couldn't give up on my children. Ellen was still in a lot of emotional pain. As I found out later it was a turning point for both Ellen and me. She realized that I did love her because I didn't give up on her in that moment. I was finally able to give her what she needed, maybe unconditional love. Isn't that the single most important characteristic of a good parent? That is the hard part— the unconditional part. Unconditional love is different from unconditional acceptance of behaviors. Fortunately, I understood that distinction as well by then.

I am not proud to say that I shuffled her off to another program. This program was comprised of psychological therapy and behavior modification. She could also get a high school diploma. Maybe she could exorcise her demons there I thought. Ellen had been the sweetest and most loving of my children. Then she became the most vicious and evil. It was almost as if someone flipped a switch in her head. It was as if she became a totally different person at around the age of twelve. I never really knew if there was a psychiatric component to her behavior since after just a few visits she refused to return to the psychologist or psychiatrist. Ellen still has not totally forgiven me for the places I forced her to go.

Around that same time, Samuel announced that he didn't want to return to military school for the next school year. He was eighteen. He had called on his eighteenth birthday from military school and announced he was leaving immediately. I was flabbergasted. I tried to talk him out of it but he wouldn't budge. My dad called him and talked to him. Between my dad, me, and some of the great teachers at the school, we were able to convince him to stay at least until the end of that semester. Now he was announcing he did not intend to return for his senior year. I'm not sure why he did not want to return. He seemed to thrive in that disciplined environment. He was getting straight As. His teachers and the administrators loved him. Since he returned home, he wasn't doing drugs or alcohol that I noticed, and I did check. I thought about his request for a few days. I knew in reality if I forced him to go back, he would just leave the school. "You can stay here on the conditions that you get your GED, work, and go to community college" I replied. Unfortunately for Samuel, this marked the beginning of many, many years of drifting aimlessly through life sometimes in the company of unsavory friends. Samuel regretted the decision not to return to military school. He told me so some years later. Samuel did get his GED. I found out later that Samuel was smoking a lot of marijuana. He dealt with things differently than Ellen. He never expressed his feelings as rage as Ellen did. He was depressed. He was simply a lost soul.

"Your children need your love the most when they deserve it the least," my dad used to always say. Maybe the same can be said of parents. By this time in our lives there had already been many years of fighting to keep my children from falling into the abyss of drugs, alcohol, and more. During this time, I struggled, long and hard, to find and know the difference between being tough and being loving. But, in the end, I realized that being tough is being loving. We all soldiered on.

My children had lost two fathers before they were out of high school. I often wondered if it was even possible to recover from that. I can't imagine the pain of that experience. I could try to empathize with their pain. But there was not much I could do. My feeling of helplessness was absolutely overwhelming. I had to watch my children act out their trauma and grief in ways that could cause injury to them and others. Even if they were spared physical injury, their conduct would certainly have long term detrimental consequences for their future. They were going to have to find their way out of this on their own. I couldn't do much of anything for them. They were hell-bent on self-destruction. I had hoped I could warehouse them somewhere safe until they were eighteen, and hopefully by then they would have healed enough to stop some of the destructive behaviors. That didn't happen. Samuel gathered up a number of DUIs, lost jobs and wasted semesters at multiple junior colleges. Ellen struggled on at the new program battling the authorities there.

Eventually Samuel simply refused to even engage in the charade that he was enrolled in and attending some classes at the local community college. He showed up for work sporadically. I would go down to his room about nine or ten a.m., demanding that he get up and go to work or class. Samuel simply rolled over and went to sleep. He got his first DUI. He spent a night or two in jail because of that. This behavior went on for a while. I hoped it was depression and he would work through it. However, he never seemed to improve.

"Samuel, you can't live here any longer," I told him one day. A friend came and picked him up. I didn't see or hear from him again for a while. This was before everyone had a cell phone. He simply disappeared. His friend was not a great guy.

I can't quite remember exactly, but I think Samuel finally called the house when my parents were there to visit for Christmas. He asked my dad to pick him up and bring him home for the holiday. Samuel stayed in his room and didn't interact with me much at all. Finally, the day arrived for my dad to drive him back to his friend's place. Samuel broke down. "I can't go back there, Mom. I haven't been able to find a job. I sleep on the floor, and I watch TV pretty much all day. I can't go back there!" My heart was breaking. I wanted to run over and hug him and tell him it was okay; he could stay with me. But I knew I had to stay strong. "What do you suggest?" I asked.

"I want to go to a community college if I can," he replied.

"Will you really go to class this time?" I asked.

"Yes. Please, Mom, give me another chance," he replied. I agreed. I was able to find a community college that he could still enroll in for the January semester. It was some eight hours away. That was a turning point. Samuel was on the road to healing. Oh, he still was not a model student, but he had definitely improved and he continued to improve.

Ellen returned from her program. She had earned a high school diploma. Ellen lived at home and attended a junior college. She graduated from the junior college and went on to attend and graduate from a four-year university. Her attitude and behavior changed for the better over time. She is still Ellen, and I still love her very much.

Jessica healed in her own way, silently. She graduated from college and moved out of state to live for a number of years. She eventually married and moved to another state. She asked me to come live near her. In time all of us, Samuel, Ellen, Gary and I moved to where Jessica was living. "I'm pregnant," Jessica announced shortly after we had all moved there.

I am amazed that my children have healed as well as they have. It has taken many, many years for them to get to this point. They are responsible for getting themselves through this. I can't take any credit. I loved them but they made the good choices and worked hard to get where they are. They deserve the credit for that.

"I have not been a very good parent," I confessed to Jessica one day after she announced she was pregnant. It had taken me months, years to get up the courage to say that to her.

"Mom, you were never a bad parent," Jessica simply said.

"Thankfully you have a poor memory," I responded. Jessica laughed and hugged me. I had similar conversations with Samuel and Ellen. My children were showing me compassion. They put themselves in my place and concluded that I had done the best I could under those very difficult circumstances. You see, my children have also learned. This was the best salve to heal my bad parenting open wound. Their compassion has continued. I can't describe how wonderful I feel when I receive compassion from my children.

I think I lacked the maturity to admit my failings earlier, but also I was afraid I would lose some of my parental authority or respect if I did. I found that admitting mistakes makes us stronger in the eyes of our children. We earn so much respect from them in doing so. Acknowledging my failings to my children and asking for their forgiveness was one of the most liberating things I have ever done. I wasn't seeking absolution from my children. Oh, they know I made huge mistakes. When they recite the stories of their childhood, there are some that cause me to cringe when I hear what I did. What Jessica meant is that she knew that I always loved her. I wanted so to be different from my mother. I never felt loved by her. That is the one gift that I wanted to give them. It seems I may have accomplished that. Somehow I believed the power of my love would pull them back to the right path. Maybe it did. Maybe it didn't. A huge element of giving them a legacy of love was showing them compassion in the difficult times in their lives. Compassion in being patient, loving, helpful but also in setting limits for them when they couldn't do it themselves.

An unimagined benefit of my admission was that they are now able to talk to me about their failings and mistakes rather than hiding them and making excuses. We can help each other because the walls have come down. We are no longer preoccupied with a futile effort to maintain a certain image with or for each other. It brought us so much closer. They showed compassion to me because they knew I was distraught over what a terrible parent I had been. They comforted me and helped me to forgive myself. I think it helped them become more forgiving of their own mistakes and faults as well and the faults and mistakes of others. They are compassionate people.

Gary got the best of all of us. Even in their darkest hours, Ellen and Samuel showed such love and generosity of spirit to Gary. It is one of the ironies of life that when we finally figure out how to be a better parent we stop having children. I was lucky to have practiced and learned a lot before I had Gary. I set firm guidelines and discipline, but he has also made good choices for himself. It is a joint effort, I think. I have had a lot of help from his siblings especially now that we live in the same neighborhood. They are a sounding board for me and for Gary. He gets lots of love and support from his family. In fact, we all do. Gary has had his struggles to process his grief, but we have all been there to show him compassion as he struggles.

"Your son is dead," the police detective told her in this gritty TV drama. They are sitting in the women's grimy apartment when she receives the news. "He has left you a lot of money. You can get out of this place and away from your abusive husband now," the detective continues. The woman is silent, staring at the floor. She shows no emotion when she is told of the money. The detective continues "You can use the money to make a better life for yourself." The woman finally speaks, "It won't bring my son back. I gave up on my son. How does a mother do that—give up on her son?" she desperately asks the detective. He of course has no answer. It is clear that nothing can erase this mother's torment and pain. I feel her pain.

I almost made the same mistake. I really didn't appreciate it when Ellen said it to me. It was one of those things the significance of which is hidden because it is said on a regular day during such a regular conversation. That is often when the most important conversations with your children take place.

"You never gave up on me," Ellen told me. "That is what got me through all of this—the fact that you never gave up on me or stopped loving me," she continued. I hugged her silently. Maybe I should forgive myself. Maybe I shouldn't see myself as a total failure as a parent after all. In spite of all my mistakes I have four wonderful children to whom I feel deeply connected. They are such loving and compassionate adults. I could not ask for any more.

We all lost so much. I lost the biggest part of myself—the shared part. Brian and I shared so many close connections—history, children, home, future plans, and feelings. For a while I lost a sense of who I was. I was forced to forge not only a new life but a new self. I lost my rock and anchor, my best friend. I lost the only person in the world for whom I was number one. Ultimately I had to and did find my way through the pain and grief in my own way and in my own time. My children did too. I have come to see Brian's illness and death as a gift that opened my eyes to how precious life is. I appreciate all that I have in ways I never did before the tragedy with Brian. I don't get angry because I don't have more or I don't have exactly what I thought I should have or what I wanted. I appreciate what is and I am thankful for it.

That is not to say that what happened to Brian wasn't abominable. I am only saying that to continue to see it only as an unimaginable tragedy limits and defines my life in a way I don't want to limit and define it. Focusing on loss and suffering leads to a life filled with bitterness and anger. Focusing on the experience as a gift leads to a life filled with gratitude, love, and compassion. A life filled with compassion and love helps create a better life for me and my family and hopefully, in some small way, a better world. Oh sure, no one can act compassionately all the time, but we can start with moments, can't we?

Through this experience I have learned not to judge others. It really is not for us, within limits, to judge if another's life or actions are right or wrong. Each of us handles things differently. Brian, the children, and I each handled his illness differently. For a while I was so arrogant as to think I was handling it better than anyone else. "They should be handling it better or they should be doing this or that," I would say to myself. I judged them all harshly. That was so wrong of me and so self-righteous! But I also have learned to not beat myself up about that either. The same question I asked myself about Brian I've had to ask myself regarding my children., i.e. how would I feel if I were in their shoes?

Culturally, we don't set ourselves up to handle difficult death or other things like addiction in a positive, caring way. I had to learn that on my own, but I want to help others see how incredibly beneficial that can be, both to themselves and to those who are hurting.

We are all still who we are, the children and I. There was no miracle transformation of any of us. We still fight and disagree. I have learned that the best way to effect change in others is to change yourself. Of course I often forget that lesson in the heat of things. We have a strong bond or connection that we all know can never be severed. People marvel at how close we all are. Maybe the bond or connection is stronger in us as a family unit because it was tested so by our circumstances. We know, first hand, its resiliency and its strength. We treasure it. We rely on it. The enjoyment of the events of life is heightened because we enjoy them together. The hardships in life are easier to bear because we face them together. Maybe this is the secret of the good marriages—the love stories as well. I never in my wildest dreams imagined this could happen to me. I felt such an emptiness, loneliness, and longing my whole life. Now I am part of a loving family. The longing is satisfied. The emptiness is gone. It can happen even for someone like me with all my problems and unhealthy and even destructive behaviors. We are truly a family. Life really doesn't get any better than this. The key to getting here was learning and practicing compassion and the forgiveness that derives from compassion. Those two things transformed us from an angry, bitter, and feuding group of people into a loving family.

As I have grown into a fuller understanding of compassion, I eventually learned to be compassionate with my parents. They are, after all, products of their own upbringings with their own childhood traumas and hurts. They did the best they knew how in raising me. When I realized all of that, I was able to have compassion for my parents. I honestly don't think they knew how to cope with all the trauma and drama of my life. It frightened them. They didn't know how to help. They coped by avoiding all of it. They intentionally structured their own lives so as to keep all events on an even keel. Everything inwardly and outwardly was to remain the same and run smoothly. They functioned best within that predictable framework. I think that is true of most of their generation. They had enough trauma with living through the Great Depression and World War II. I can understand that now. By seeing things from my parents' perspective I was able to stop judging and criticizing them. I was able to have compassion for them and to forgive them. They did the best they could.

As I grew to understand my parent's early lives better, I was able to forgive them. Forgiving them showed me the way to forgiving myself regarding my treatment of my own children. I made very selfish choices that hurt my children terribly. But as my parents did with me, I did the best I could in raising my children.

I am amazed that my children have shown me compassion and forgiven me for all my mistake and failings as a parent. Perhaps they saw me show compassion for my parents and my parents show compassion for others and modeled that. Perhaps they realized that I did the best I could. Certainly their experience with Brian's illness caused them to want to be and to develop into compassionate people.

Compassion was the key to not only surviving this experience but also to healing, growing and even flourishing. These experiences just as easily could have torn my children and I apart. But instead of blaming, criticizing, judging, and hating, we learned to have compassion for and to forgive each other and ourselves.

When we show and/or receive compassion we also forge bonds with others. We connect with each other. I don't understand the exact mechanism for this, but I know it happens because it has happened in my own family. It is part of the magic of compassion.

Compassion is not just a feeling. It is also the act of actively showing you care by helping and doing. Compassion has worked its magic in my life. It continues to work magic in my life every day. It was a long arduous journey to find this path. It wasn't without pain, but we all have adversity in our lives. We all experience pain, hardship, and loss. But when you allow compassion to enter in, it can sooth the hurt and sorrow. It can help you find a path to a more fulfilling and happier life.

POSTSCRIPT

A Tribute to a Compassionate Life?

WE CAN SO EASILY BECOME COMPLACENT AND ARROGANT IN OUR lives. We are bombarded with advertisements and other messages that we deserve the best, that we are or can be better than others and that people are solely responsible for and must be blamed for their own misery and problems. We must compete with each other and as such we must strive to pursue our own individual interests to get ahead. We mistakenly believe in survival of the fittest. We believe we don't want or need others, except occasionally, and to be used for our own ends. We don't believe in community just for the sake of community. I call this individualism run amok or pathological individualism. It is a world where compassion is pity and relegated solely to our sporadic community service activities or church. But what would happen if we rejected those cultural beliefs and instead saw our daily interactions with everyone we encountered as an opportunity to show compassion? What would our lives and our world look like then?

As I was finishing this manuscript, I had perhaps the saddest yet most profound experience of my life. It showed me just how powerful compassion is, and it allowed me to forgive—and love—my father even more than I ever thought possible.

It was one of those days when I forgot the lessons that I had learned. I still have those days! I just felt irritable, crabby, like the whole world was against me and nothing would ever be right or good in my life. I have no idea where that comes from even though I have been prone to depression all my life. I'm not talking about the extreme clinical depression, just that feeling that nothing good would ever really happen for me. I was somehow doomed by the universe to unhappiness or lack of success or anything else that would elevate me out of my perceived mundaneness or desperation of my everyday life. Would I ever get to where I wanted to be in all or maybe just any aspect of my life—love, financial security, career recognition. And then I would feel guilty because I am a very lucky woman. That whole battle was raging and I was rude and inconsiderate to everyone I met that day. I couldn't seem to stop myself. Sometimes this just overtakes me for no discernible reason, and other times it is a result of being at the tail end of a difficult time.

After the dark mood passed I really got to thinking about how I had treated the people I came into contact with during that time. I certainly didn't brighten their day, but how awful had I been? I know how it effects my mood when someone is crabby to me at the checkout or how much better I feel when I get a smile and a thank you. We are always looking for the big acts, but it really is the little acts of kindness, thoughtfulness that count. I learned that first from my dad.

"Why don't you go over and pick up Dad for brunch?" I asked my sister. It was about ten o'clock a.m. on a Sunday, and I was finishing up a phone call. "I'll be ready when you get back here to pick me up," I said. My parents and I lived in the same neighborhood. They had just moved to a house a few blocks away from mine about seven months prior. My mom was not living at the house at the time, so we were only picking up my dad. I was so looking forward to spending some time with him on a Sunday when I wasn't preoccupied with work appointments or projects. We didn't often get a chance to go to brunch together, just the three of us, because my sister lives in another state. It was a real treat!

As I was finishing up my phone call I saw my sister was trying to call me. "I'll call her back in a minute," I thought, as I really didn't want to interrupt the person who was talking to me. "She's calling about something Dad was wearing or a delay in going to brunch," I thought to myself.

Just a minute or two later, my front door burst open and my sister ran in shrieking, "Hang up the phone! Dad fell down the stairs. He's dead!" I dropped the phone. We ran over to my parents' house. Action has always been good at keeping my feelings at bay. The police had already arrived.

"What's your name?" my dad asked the server. She had stopped quickly to ask us what we wanted to drink. The restaurant was packed at the peak of the lunch hour, and the server was running everywhere.

"Oh God!" I thought to myself. "Here he goes again, bothering very busy people." To tell the truth, I was embarrassed. Didn't my dad notice that this server was running around like a chicken with her head cut off? Older people don't seem to be aware of how busy the younger generations are!

"My name is Morgan," the server said as she scampered away.

"What was her name?" my dad asked me.

"Morgan," I replied.

The server returned to our table to take our order.

"How do you spell your name?" my dad asked her. She had to spell it a few times before my dad actually got it.

"Where are you from, Morgan?" he asked her. I put my head into my hands and silently groaned.

"I'm from here," she replied.

"Well, it is nice to meet you," my dad said, extending his hand. He had a few questions about the menu and then she took our order.

"I'm glad that is over," I said to myself. "Maybe she can get back to work now."

"Are you in school, Morgan?" my dad asked when she came back to deliver our meals. "What is your major?" he asked. "How long have you worked here?" he continued. Morgan proceeded to tell Dad a little about herself and then actually seemed to regret having to leave to take care of another table. Truth be told, my dad's niceties only took a few minutes even though it seemed like an eternity to me. When things slowed down, Morgan came back over and chatted with my dad for a little bit longer. She smiled and waved when we left.

It takes time to care, and in our busy lives we often don't take or make time to treat others with care and compassion.

"Did your dad have any health issues?" the coroner asked my sister and I as we waited outside of the house for them to remove my dad's body.

"None," I replied. "He didn't take any medications and had no health issues whatsoever. He was driving, gardening, volunteering, and visiting my mom every day," I replied.

"Because he was a perfectly healthy person who died unexpectedly, we are going to have to conduct a full autopsy," the medical examiner said. "We have to rule out any foul play." He wasn't asking our permission, just letting us know the procedure very matter-of-factly. I couldn't even think about my dad's body being dissected and examined.

"Dad, let's go to lunch downtown today," I suggested.

"That sounds great," my dad replied. "Because our neighbor is the manager at an establishment downtown, and I would like to eat lunch there." I was a bit annoyed because when we got downtown, we spent a good bit of time looking for this place.

As we struggled to find this place, I finally said to Dad, "The neighbor really doesn't care if we patronize his business or not." I actually felt pretty awful saying that to my dad. However, I often felt like my dad did not really understand the way the current world worked. He was eighty-nine years old, after all. Dad didn't reply to my comment. We finally found the place, and I parked illegally while Dad ran in to see if the place was open.

"It is only a bar," my dad said, sounding very disappointed. "It is important that we support our neighbors," he said as we drove to another restaurant. That may have been the way things worked when he was young or I was a kid but certainly not now. That neighbor moved out of the apartment just a few weeks later, so my dad never got a chance to tell him we tried to find his restaurant. He only lived there for a few months.

My dad's behavior often embarrassed me. But why? What's so embarrassing? Is it really embarrassing to show we care about our neighbors, servers in restaurants, or people we encounter in our daily lives? Does it make us appear weak, needy, or not busy enough in our own lives? Maybe I was afraid it made me appear vulnerable to someone else if that person didn't respond positively to my offer to connect.

As I observe other people, I don't think I am the only who feels embarrassed. What is it about our culture that causes us to be embarrassed when a stranger takes the time to show they care with small gestures of kindness or consideration? Heck, people don't even say please, thank you, or hold open doors for each other anymore. When was the last time a driver waved you a thank you when you let them into the traffic stream, etc.? We don't acknowledge others or their acts of kindness and what does that say about us as a culture?

My parents had moved from Pittsburgh to Texas. My mom had a bad fall and had broken her femur. The move was precipitated by her health combined with some very harsh winters. The house was getting to be too much to take care of financially and physically for my parents. My mom had lived in the Pittsburgh area all her life, so to say she was unhappy about the move would be a real understatement. It is hard to describe her level of anger and resentment.

"Dad, let's just buy some new furniture when you get here," I said as we discussed the logistics of the move from Pennsylvania to Texas.

"Your mother wants to bring all the furniture," he replied.

"Not that couch!" I exclaimed, horrified. "It is so beat up, and it won't fit anywhere in the apartment," I stated matter-of-factly. "It is going to cost more to move the stuff than it will cost to buy new furniture," I argued. My parents had owned all their furniture for more than forty years. The couch was given to my parents by my aunt in 1970. "My poor dad," I later thought. He was in the middle between my mother and me as perhaps he had been so many times before. The couch and everything else came to Austin.

It was embarrassing as a kid. Our house was shabby—both the furniture and the general condition. As a child, it made me angry that my parents didn't work harder to have a nicer house or to provide nicer things for us kids. Later, at my dad's memorial service held in Pittsburgh, I truly came to appreciate the valuable lesson of their lives and the immeasurable legacy they left to their family and others.

Right after my parents moved to Austin, my dad was giving me a tour of their apartment, which he loved to do. Their decorating style, especially as they grew older, consisted of the furniture they had for forty years in its original form coupled with mementos from their lives hung on the walls. I think it made my parents feel at home as their living space told the story of their lives. "What's this?" I asked, looking at a photograph of my parents that looked like it had appeared in a newspaper. It was hanging on a wall in the very back bedroom. I was thinking it was one of those things you can order online they received maybe as a gift from someone.

"Oh, that is something that appeared in the Pittsburgh newspaper," my dad responded as he tried to lead me past the place the photo was hanging. I stopped to read the newspaper article. The headline read "Community Champions," then a photo of my parents. Underneath the photo, it said in bold print my parents' names and "Volunteers making a world of difference." The article was short but talked about some of the volunteer work my parents had been involved in for the past twenty-plus years.

"Dad, I didn't know anything about this. Why didn't you tell me?" I chastised him. My dad didn't say anything. I never really did find out much about the award. I think they had a dinner to honor my parents, but since I didn't know anything I did not attend. I was very sad I missed an opportunity to share in the life of my parents.

My parents' generation was raised to be humble and modest. Your good deeds and good life would speak for themselves. We have become such shameless self-promoters and braggarts. Our excuse is that we have to do it in order to get ahead in the business world. Do we really? Current evidence would suggest naught. Admittedly my parents were part of a long standing community where their deeds would be recognized and appreciated. In our transient society, that is not the case but still, shouldn't good deeds be unspoken? Are we doing them to do a good deed or to receive recognition? My parents never ever spoke of all their good deeds and works. I knew my parents devoted the latter part of their lives to doing volunteer work but I didn't know the extent of it until my dad's memorial service.

"Oh my God! I can't believe your father has passed," I heard some strange voice on the other end of the phone say.

"Who is this?" of course I asked.

"This is Larry." Sob.

I had heard my dad refer generally to Larry, but I had never spoken to Larry, and I didn't know much about him other than he was someone my dad had befriended while living in Pittsburgh. "Your dad was like a father to me." Sob. "He was the first person in my life who believed in me." Sob. "Because of him and his belief in me, I was able to get off the streets, get a job, get married, and start a family." Sob. "He never gave up on me even when everyone else did." Uncontrollable sobbing. "I can't talk anymore," he said and passed the phone to another stranger.

"What are we going to do without him?" a woman said into the phone.

"I don't know," I said.

"Who would like to come up and share something about Bob?" the minister who was presiding over my dad's memorial service asked the attendees. To my surprise there was a line of people who wanted to say something.

A middle-aged black man was the first to speak. "You know Bob worked with the homeless men in this area. He helped run the worship service held here in the church. He helped serve breakfast to the men. He helped establish a small shelter here at the church and helped to run that. But he did so much more than that. He attended the church service for the homeless men every Sunday. At the end of every service, he would stand at the door. As each person arrived at the exit door, Bob would look into his eyes and shake his hand. He would ask how you were doing. He would give words of encouragement and sometimes even give everyone a few bucks. But the biggest gift Bob gave was a genuine concern that was not contaminated with judgment, criticism, pity, or a feeling of his superiority. Bob has been gone from Pittsburgh for over five years, and do you know men on the street will still come up to me and ask me how Bob is doing? He had infinite patience and never gave up on us when almost everyone else did."

A well-dressed, middle-aged white man was the next to speak. "When I first met Bob, I was not a good giver. I would judge or criticize those in need rather than just doing or giving what was needed. Bob made me want to be a better person, and from him I learned to give."

Others spoke saying wonderful things about my dad—how he was a good neighbor, a good friend who always was ready, willing, and committed to helping. One woman spoke of being evicted from her low-income apartment and how my dad spent countless hours finding her a new, affordable place to live. Without his help she would have ended up living on the streets she said. You see, my parents had joined this church because it was an inner-city church and it ministered to the neediest in our society, including the homeless.

But perhaps the story told by the minister was the most powerful. As she told it: One day a homeless person managed to get past the ushers in the narthex and somehow made it all the way to the front of the church during Sunday worship. He was barefoot and was not wearing a shirt. He sat down at the very front of the church. There was panic in the church and the parishioners could hear the ushers discussing frantically what they should do. As everyone stared incredulous and as the ushers debated what to do, my dad walked to the front of the church. He took off his jacket and put it on the homeless man. He took off his shoes and gave them to him, and then gently led him away to the area of the church where the homeless ministry was located.

The people, including the minister, glowed as they told of their experiences with my dad. They cried as they related how he had stood by them through some very difficult times in their lives. They described how Dad had changed them and their lives forever. It was the magic of compassion again. My dad's life is a testament to that. How many lives had he touched and changed for the better? I will never know. But the number, in the end, doesn't matter. What does is that he gave himself over to a life of compassion, and those he touched, including me, are all much better human beings because of it.

Certain organizations are currently in the process of working to scientifically measure the benefits of compassion to show us it is good for us. You know the benefits if you have ever shown compassion—given freely without judgment and without expecting anything in return or receiving anything in return. You have experienced the powerful connection it creates between you and another being. That connection reaches inside each of us and sends a warm feeling to the deepest recesses of our beings.

We feel a warm physical sensation as a feeling of peace and love spreads over us. Compassion heals wounds. It is a source of hope and inspiration in what can otherwise be a very bleak world or situation. It transforms us both—the giver and the recipient.

My dad loved to quote St. Francis of Assisi, "It is in giving that we receive." Compassion reminds us that we need each other and that we are, when at our best, part of a compassionate, caring community.

I was ashamed of myself that at times I had been angry and resentful that my parents did not plan better so as to have the resources to care for themselves in their elder years and instead had to look to their children for financial assistance. At the memorial service, all the anger and resentment fell away. Neither of my parents had any desire for material wealth. They genuinely sought to expend their efforts not on amassing material things but in helping others. I saw the richness of their lives and their legacy at that moment. My dad had always taught me to find pleasure in the simple things in life that have nothing to do with money—nature, family, good friends, community and, of course, helping others who are less fortunate.

"Bob has appeared at the pearly gates to meet his maker, and God has said, "Well done my son, well done," " the minister said as she closed her homily. There was not a dry eye in the church. I could hear the sobs behind me.

What we are here to do? Only you can answer that for yourself. But I do know that we are not here to judge, criticize, blame, or compete with one another. We are most definitely not here to amass material wealth—just look at those who spend their lives chasing nothing but the almighty dollar. Where has our society's focus on amassing material wealth gotten us? What you do influences who you are. If we show compassion to one another, we form communities bound together by our acts of love and kindness. That enriches all of our lives

My grandmother used to say, "To those to whom much is given, much is required." But who are we required to help, we often ask ourselves. Everyone would be the answer according to my dad. There is always someone who is worse off than us and needs our help. My dad used to say, "I felt sorry for myself because I had no shoes until I saw a man who had no feet."

Truly no matter where we are in our life there is someone who has less than us. We all have much to give and it starts with just asking ourselves in our daily interactions "How would I feel if I were in his/her shoes or if I were that person?" The actions will then naturally follow and compassion will work its magic.

As my dad's journey through this life came to an end, I could see how far my journey had taken me. He had learned the lessons of love, forgiveness, and compassion and put them into practice every day of his life. I wish I had known more of what he did for others. But he was so very modest. He didn't talk about it. He did not believe in receiving accolades for helping others. The point was to help others, not to receive credit and praise for doing so. He believed in leading by example. I do wonder how I would have fared through my trials had he shared more with me, but then my dad, as we all are, was a work in progress. And often it is hardest to show compassion to those to whom we are closest. I am in awe of the way my dad lived his life especially knowing how he grew up.

My dad's life, especially in his later years, was always an inspiration to me even without knowing the full extent of the compassionate life he led. I could see that people he encountered, in his daily life, felt that he was interested in them and cared about them. At his memorial service, there was an overwhelming feeling of warmth and love in the church as people spoke glowingly about what my dad had done for them and how much that meant to them, even changing the course of many of their lives. He built relationships and communities through his practice of compassion. He loved and was beloved. As my son-in-law so aptly put it, "He left the world a better place for having been here."

I am in awe of the way my dad lived his life. Somewhere along his journey he learned the magic of compassion and made it part of his daily life. One of the materially successful attendees at the memorial service said, "That was impressive." Perhaps my dad has, posthumously, inspired him to practice compassion daily in everything he does.

But now I can and will focus my life on helping others to find the beauty and magic of compassion in their lives. I think it is the most fitting tribute to my father and a way to honor my own experiences too.

My hope for you is that you find ways to make compassion part of your journey and daily life. Imagine how it would feel if rather than judging, blaming, competing with, and condemning others, we work to alleviate the suffering, troubles, and problems of others by being caring and helpful. Imagine a world where we all show compassion every day toward others and in everything we do. That would be magic.

About the Author

Virginia Hunter Sampson

THE AUTHOR IS A SINGLE PARENT OF FOUR grown children and a grandmother of three (and counting). After losing her husband to Lou Gehrig's disease, she raised her four children as a single mother. She was inspired to write Compassion Magic and her children's book, Superhero Sam Saves His Family, as a result of her own struggle to find compassion in her life and to raise compassionate and throughful children in a world that seems to be imbused with an atmosphere of selfishness and narcissism.

www.ingramcontent.com/pod-product-compliance
Lightning Source LLC
Chambersburg PA
CBHW021505090426
42739CB00007B/468